P9-CFC-637

DEMCO

THE
HISTORY
OF
ISSUES

The Death Penalty

THE
HISTORY
OF
ISSUES

The Death Penalty

Jean Alicia Elster, *Book Editor*

Bruce Glassman, *Vice President*
Bonnie Szumski, *Publisher*
Helen Cothran, *Managing Editor*

GREENHAVEN PRESS
An imprint of Thomson Gale, a part of The Thomson Corporation

THOMSON

GALE

Detroit • New York • San Francisco • San Diego • New Haven, Conn.
Waterville, Maine • London • Munich

© 2005 Thomson Gale, a part of The Thomson Corporation.

Thomson and Star Logo are trademarks and Gale and Greenhaven Press are registered trademarks used herein under license.

For more information, contact
Greenhaven Press
27500 Drake Rd.
Farmington Hills, MI 48331-3535
Or you can visit our Internet site at http://www.gale.com

LIBRARY OF CONGRESS CATALOGING-IN-PUBLICATION DATA

The death penalty / Jean Alicia Elster, book editor.
   p. cm. — (The history of issues)
Includes bibliographical references and index.
ISBN 0-7377-1911-7 (lib. : alk. paper) — ISBN 0-7377-1912-5 (pbk. : alk. paper)
   1. Capital punishment—United States—History. I. Elster, Jean Alicia. II. Series.
KF9227.C2D4116 2005
345.73'0773—dc22   2004043661

Printed in the United States of America

Contents

Chapter 1: Is the Death Penalty Cruel and Unusual Punishment?

1. Electrocution Is Not Cruel and Unusual Punishment

by Melville Weston Fuller

The 1890 U.S. Supreme Court ruling in *Kemmler* confirms the New York state legislature's determination that death by electrocution is a just and fair punishment.

2. The Death Penalty Is Not as Cruel and Unusual as Life Imprisonment

by Jacques Barzun

In an article written in 1962, the author supports the death penalty by describing the barbarism of life imprisonment.

3. The Death Penalty Is Cruel and Unusual Punishment

by William O. Douglas and William J. Brennan Jr.

In the 1972 landmark case of *Furman v. Georgia*, the U.S. Supreme Court ruled that the death penalty violates the Eighth Amendment's cruel and unusual clause and is therefore unconstitutional.

4. The Death Penalty Is Not Always Cruel and Unusual Punishment

by Potter Stewart

In 1976 the U.S. Supreme Court upheld a death

sentence in *Gregg v. Georgia*, overturning the 1972 case of *Furman v. Georgia*, which had held that the death penalty was cruel and unusual.

Chapter 2: The Deterrence Debate

Chapter 3: Fairness and the Death Penalty

defendants will inevitably be convicted and
executed if the state of New York reinstates its
capital punishment laws.

Chapter 4: Moral Issues

Foreword

In the 1940s, at the height of the Holocaust, Jews struggled to create a nation of their own in Palestine, a region of the Middle East that at the time was controlled by Britain. The British had placed limits on Jewish immigration to Palestine, hampering efforts to provide refuge to Jews fleeing the Holocaust. In response to this and other British policies, an underground Jewish resistance group called Irgun began carrying out terrorist attacks against British targets in Palestine, including immigration, intelligence, and police offices. Most famously, the group bombed the King David Hotel in Jerusalem, the site of a British military headquarters. Although the British were warned well in advance of the attack, they failed to evacuate the building. As a result, ninety-one people were killed (including fifteen Jews) and forty-five were injured.

Early in the twentieth century, Ireland, which had long been under British rule, was split into two countries. The south, populated mostly by Catholics, eventually achieved independence and became the Republic of Ireland. Northern Ireland, mostly Protestant, remained under British control. Catholics in both the north and south opposed British control of the north, and the Irish Republican Army (IRA) sought unification of Ireland as an independent nation. In 1969, the IRA split into two factions. A new radical wing, the Provisional IRA, was created and soon undertook numerous terrorist bombings and killings throughout Northern Ireland, the Republic of Ireland, and even in England. One of its most notorious attacks was the 1974 bombing of a Birmingham, England, bar that killed nineteen people.

In the mid-1990s, an Islamic terrorist group called al Qaeda began carrying out terrorist attacks against American targets overseas. In communications to the media, the organization listed several complaints against the United States. It generally opposed all U.S. involvement and presence in the Middle East. It particularly objected to the presence of U.S. troops in Saudi Arabia, which is the home of several Islamic holy sites. And it strongly condemned the United States for supporting the nation of Israel, which it claimed was an oppressor of Muslims. In 1998 al Qaeda's leaders issued a fatwa (a religious legal statement) calling for Muslims to kill Americans. Al Qaeda acted on this order many times—most memorably on September 11, 2001, when it attacked the World Trade Center and the Pentagon, killing nearly three thousand people.

These three groups—Irgun, the Provisional IRA, and al Qaeda—have achieved varied results. Irgun's terror campaign contributed to Britain's decision to pull out of Palestine and to support the creation of Israel in 1948. The Provisional IRA's tactics kept pressure on the British, but they also alienated many would-be supporters of independence for Northern Ireland. Al Qaeda's attacks provoked a strong U.S. military response but did not lessen America's involvement in the Middle East nor weaken its support of Israel. Despite these different results, the means and goals of these groups were similar. Although they emerged in different parts of the world during different eras and in support of different causes, all three had one thing in common: They all used clandestine violence to undermine a government they deemed oppressive or illegitimate.

The destruction of oppressive governments is not the only goal of terrorism. For example, terror is also used to minimize dissent in totalitarian regimes and to promote extreme ideologies. However, throughout history the motivations of terrorists have been remarkably similar, proving the old adage that "the more things change, the more they remain the same." Arguments for and against terrorism thus boil down to the same set of universal arguments regardless of the age: Some argue that terrorism is justified to change (or, in the case of state terror, to maintain) the prevailing political order; others respond that terrorism is inhumane and unacceptable under any circumstances. These basic views transcend time and place.

Similar fundamental arguments apply to other controversial social issues. For instance, arguments over the death penalty have always featured competing views of justice. Scholars cite biblical texts to claim that a person who takes a life must forfeit his or her life, while others cite religious doctrine to support their view that only God can take a human life. These arguments have remained essentially the same throughout the centuries. Likewise, the debate over euthanasia has persisted throughout the history of Western civilization. Supporters argue that it is compassionate to end the suffering of the dying by hastening their impending death; opponents insist that it is society's duty to make the dying as comfortable as possible as death takes its natural course.

Greenhaven Press's The History of Issues series illustrates this constancy of arguments surrounding major social issues. Each volume in the series focuses on one issue—including terrorism, the death penalty, and euthanasia—and examines how the debates have both evolved and remained essentially the same over the years. Primary documents such as newspaper articles, speeches, and government reports illuminate historical developments and offer perspectives from throughout history. Secondary sources provide overviews and commentaries from a more contemporary perspective. An introduction begins each anthology and supplies essential context and background. An annotated table of contents, chronology, and index allow for easy reference, and a bibliography and list of organizations to contact point to additional sources of information on the book's topic. With these features, The History of Issues series permits readers to glimpse both the historical and contemporary dimensions of humanity's most pressing and controversial social issues.

Introduction

Since the colonial period Americans have sought humane ways to execute those in society who have been convicted of capital crimes. Many different ways of carrying out capital sentences in individual states have been tried and abandoned. Initially, public hanging was the dominant punishment for capital crimes—a practice that was brought from England and adopted by the colonies in the 1600s. By the beginning of the twenty-first century, hanging, firing squad, electrocution, lethal gas, and lethal injection were the five modes of execution available to the thirty-eight states with statutes allowing the death penalty. As legal scholar Deborah W. Denno writes, although legislators chose these methods "to ensure greater humaneness . . . for those who will be executed, each of them at some point has been labeled barbaric, inhumane, and unfit to be used to carry out state-sanctioned death sentences."[1]

Colonial Methods of Execution

The early colonists used hanging because it was, according to historian Stuart Banner, "the ancient and familiar English method of executing criminals."[2] In keeping with that Anglo-Saxon model, hangings were staged as public spectacles. Children were brought by their parents to witness the convicted person's death. Crowds, sometimes numbering in the thousands, gathered around the gallows. Often, the condemned was slowly transported to the execution site in plain view of all, so that even those who did not wish to witness the execution were aware of the impending death. As Banner writes, "Condemned criminals were well aware that their role at an execution was to be seen by as many as possible."[3] A sermon was often given at the gallows, and the condemned often made a speech. Executions were publicly performed because they were intended to deter potential criminals and to impress upon young people the consequences of committing crime.

Although the colonists used hanging as their main method of capital punishment, they sometimes used other forms of execution, particularly when killing those accused of being witches. The one recorded instance of someone being "pressed" to death was in 1692 during the witch trials in Salem, Massachusetts. Pressing involved placing weights or stones upon the person's chest until he or she died. More commonly, however, suspected or convicted witches were burned to death. In addition, until the mid–eighteenth century, rebellious slaves were sometimes burned at the stake. However, by the time of the American Revolution execution by burning was considered inhumane and barbaric.

Early American Hangings

At the time of the ratification of the U.S. Constitution in 1789, the only acceptable mode of execution in the United States was hanging. Yet while hangings were accepted, public hangings were falling into disfavor. Beginning in the late 1700s and continuing until his death in 1813, Benjamin Rush—a physician, legal scholar, and death penalty abolitionist—lectured across the country and wrote widely against public hangings and for a more humane criminal justice system. He won a great deal of support for his position. The drunkenness and loud, riotous behavior that often accompanied these executions also fueled the call by officials for an end to public hangings. By 1835 the state of New York had enacted the first law against public hangings, mandating that executions be held in a prison yard behind a wall or a fence and viewed only by "official" witnesses. Several states followed suit, but change occurred slowly: It was not until one hundred years later, in Missouri, that the last public hanging was carried out in America.

Blood Atonement and the Firing Squad

By the late 1800s hanging was still the main method of execution. However, in keeping with the Mormon concept of blood atonement for sins, Utah had provided for death by firing squad since territorial days in 1854. Death by shooting did, indeed, cause the condemned to shed blood as part of the execution. However, many people considered the procedure inhumane because of the damage done to the condemned's body during the execution. Nonetheless, condemned convicts in that state continued to have the option of death by firing squad until 2004, when the governor of Utah signed legislation abolishing it as a means of execution. Nevada also began to offer inmates the choice of firing squad or hanging beginning in 1911, but only one inmate chose the firing squad before the state switched to lethal gas in 1924.

The Development of the Electric Chair

Although hanging remained the main method of execution at the end of the nineteenth century, critics of death by hanging had begun to assert that capital punishment should be made less painful for the condemned. As Banner describes, the nature of hanging and the variations caused by "the height of the drop, the elasticity of the rope, the position of the knot, the weather, the tension in the condemned person's neck muscles, and not least the skills of the hangman"[4] meant that it was virtually impossible to insure a painless death by this method of execution. As a result, the governor of the state of New York created a commission to find a more humane method of execution than death by hanging. The commission recommended death by electrocution as the most humane method of execution available to modern society. Based upon that recommendation, the first electric chair was built in New York in 1888, and William Kemmler became the first person scheduled to be executed by electrocution in 1890. However, before his execution, his case and pending electrocution were appealed to the U.S. Supreme Court. The Court deferred to the decision of the New York state legislature to adopt electrocution as a means of execution. It also ruled that capital punishment does not violate the Constitution's Eighth Amendment provision against cruel and unusual punishment. The death sentence proceeded as scheduled.

Witnesses to Kemmler's execution reported that the executioner botched the first application of electric current and had to apply the current a second time. In addition, the condemned's body was grossly mutilated. They described death by electrocution as being more inhumane than hanging. In spite of such pronouncements, electrocution soon became a popular means of execution in other states. By 1913 thirteen states were using electrocution in executions because they believed that electrocution was less painful and more humane than hanging.

Introducing Death by Lethal Gas

As the debate over electrocutions continued in the late 1800s, some medical practitioners began to argue that death by lethal gas would be a more humane form of execution than death by electricity. With the increased occurrence of botched electrocutions, more state legislatures began approving execution by lethal gas rather than by electrocution. Nevada was the first state to choose lethal gas as the means of state executions in 1924. By the early 1970s twelve other states had followed Nevada's example and selected death by lethal gas as the preferred method of execution. However, many people did not believe that lethal gas was a humane means of execution for condemned prisoners. Witnesses to some of these deaths describe them with horror. As former San Quentin prison warden Clifton Duffy reported, "The eyes pop. The skin turns purple and the victim begins to drool."[5] And Richard Traystman, a doctor at Johns Hopkins University School of Medicine, writes that a person being executed by lethal gas is "unquestionably experiencing pain and extreme anxiety."[6] As of 2002 only Arizona, California, Missouri, and Wyoming authorized the use of lethal gas in executions.

Death by Lethal Injection

Lethal injection became the preferred method of execution in the late twentieth century after the first execution by this means took place in Texas in 1982. Requiring only syringes, intravenous tubes, and three chemicals, lethal injection was inexpensive. It was also deemed to be painless because the condemned is supposedly rendered unconscious by the introduction of the first of the three chemicals injected. Witnesses to these executions pronounce them less gruesome than the other methods. However, Banner argues that lethal injection is not as pain free as commonly believed, writing that some inmates have "violent physical reactions to the chemicals, gasping and choking in their final minutes."[7] As of 2004, suits were still being filed in state courts alleging that the initial chemical injected does not render the condemned unconscious but rather paralyzes the muscles so that the person cannot speak while still being able to feel excruciating pain.

Despite these concerns, the most widely used form of execution today is lethal injection. Of the thirty-eight states with statutes allowing the death penalty, thirty-seven authorize this method. In the few states with more than one authorized method, prisoners may choose the way they wish to be executed. Nebraska is the only state that requires electrocution as its sole form of execution.

More than three hundred years after the first protests against public hangings, people are still debating and speaking out against the various methods of capital punishment. Society continues to seek a humane means of execution but disagrees about what form it should take. Some people further argue that executions can never be humane and that capital punishment is wrong. The debate over methods of execution is only one of the issues that has been important in the history of capital punishment.

The volume *History of Issues: The Death Penalty* examines many topics that have been central in the history of capital punishment in America, including cruel and unusual punishment, deterrence, and race and gender discrimination, as well as issues of fairness and morality.

Notes

1. Deborah W. Denno, "Execution and the Forgotten Eighth Amendment," in James R. Acker, Robert M. Bohn, and Charles S. Lanier, eds., *America's Experiment with Capital Punishment: Reflections on the Past, Present, and Future of the Ultimate Penal Sanction.* Durham, NC: Carolina Academic Press, 1998, p. 567.
2. Stuart Banner, *The Death Penalty: An American History.* Cambridge, MA: Harvard University Press, 2002, p. 44.
3. Banner, *The Death Penalty*, p. 11.
4. Banner, *The Death Penalty*, pp. 170–71.
5. Quoted in J. Weisberg, "This Is Your Death," *New Republic*, July 1, 1991.
6. Quoted in Weisberg, "This Is Your Death."
7. Banner, *The Death Penalty*, pp. 297–98.

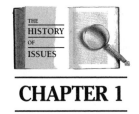

THE
HISTORY
OF
ISSUES

CHAPTER 1

Is the Death Penalty Cruel and Unusual Punishment?

Chapter Preface

The Eighth Amendment of the U.S. Constitution—which includes a prohibition against cruel and unusual punishment—was ratified by the states in 1791. Since that time people have debated and continue to disagree about what kind of penalty actually constitutes cruel and unusual punishment.

When the framers of the Constitution proscribed cruel and unusual punishment, they had in mind barbarous acts of punishment such as piling stones upon the condemned person's chest and "pressing" him or her to death or burning accused witches at the stake. During the nineteenth century some people began to argue that the prevailing method of inflicting death in capital cases, public hanging, was cruel and unusual punishment. Gradually, states enacted laws against the practice. As the twentieth century progressed, judgments about what constitutes cruel and unusual punishment began to take into account factors beyond the physical method of execution. These factors included the length of time from sentencing to execution, racial bias against the accused, and the possibility of convicting the innocent.

In 1972 the U.S. Supreme Court made a landmark ruling on what is considered cruel and unusual punishment under law. In *Furman v. Georgia*, the Court ruled that a punishment is cruel and unusual if it is too severe for the crime, if it is arbitrary, if it offends society's sense of justice, and if it is not more effective than a less severe penalty. The Court held that Georgia's death penalty statute, which gave the jury complete sentencing discretion, could result in arbitrary sentencing and was therefore cruel and unusual. The Court's ruling voided death penalty statutes in forty states and commuted the sentences of 629 death row inmates around the country. States began to rewrite their statutes to eliminate the breaches to the Eighth Amendment cited in *Furman*.

In the years since the *Furman* ruling, two of the major debates over whether the death penalty is cruel and unusual have centered on the execution of the mentally ill or retarded and the execution of juveniles. In 1986 the Supreme Court ruled in *Ford v. Wainwright* that insane people cannot be executed. However, it went on to rule in 1989 in *Penry v. Lynaugh* that executing people with mental retardation does not violate the Eighth Amendment. In the case of juveniles, the Court also ruled in 1989 that the Eighth Amendment does not prohibit the death penalty for crimes committed at age sixteen or seventeen. Nonetheless, fifteen states today bar the execution of anyone who was younger than eighteen at the time of his or her crime.

Although debate over whether the death penalty is cruel and unusual continues to be heated, according to a 2004 Harris Poll, more than two-thirds of Americans support the punishment for serious crimes. However, almost everyone polled said they believed that the innocent are sometimes executed, which indicates that many people still have grave doubts about how arbitrary the penalty remains.

Electrocution Is Not Cruel and Unusual Punishment

MELVILLE WESTON FULLER

In 1885, in a message to the state legislature, the governor of New York described the practice of execution by hanging as barbaric. Looking for a more humane way to carry out death sentences, in 1888 the New York legislature passed the Electrical Execution Act. In 1889, William Kemmler was convicted of murder in the state of New York and sentenced to death by electrocution. His sentence was appealed to the U.S. Supreme Court. At issue was the question of whether death by electrocution as mandated by the state statute violates the cruel and unusual punishment clause of the Eighth Amendment of the U.S. Constitution. In the following extract from the case, the Court holds that the Eighth Amendment does not apply to the states. In addition, the Court defers to the state legislature's determination that death by electrocution is not cruel and unusual punishment. The author of this decision, Melville Weston Fuller, was chief justice of the U.S. Supreme Court from 1888 to 1910.

Copies of the indictment of [William] Kemmler, otherwise called Hort, for the murder of Matilda Zeigler, otherwise called Matilda Hort; the judgment and sentence of the court; and the warrant to the warden to execute the sentence, were attached to the petition and returned. The

Melville Weston Fuller, opinion, *In re Kemmler*, U.S. Supreme Court, 1890.

conclusion of the warrant, pursuing the sentence, was in the words: "Now, therefore, you are hereby ordered, commanded and required to execute the said sentence upon him, the said William Kemmler, otherwise called John Hort, upon some day within the week commencing on Monday, the 24th day of June, in the year of our Lord one thousand eight hundred and eighty-nine, and within the walls of Auburn State Prison [in New York], or within the yard or enclosure adjoining thereto, by then and there causing to pass through the body of him, the said William Kemmler, otherwise called John Hort, a current of electricity of sufficient intensity to cause death, and that the application of such current of electricity be continued until he, the said William Kemmler, otherwise called John Hort, be dead."

History of State Appeals

Upon the return of the writ [of error] before the county judge, counsel for the petitioner offered to prove that the infliction of death by the application of electricity as directed "is a cruel and unusual punishment, within the meaning of the Constitution, and that it cannot, therefore, be lawfully inflicted, and to establish the facts upon which the court can pass, as to the character of the penalty. The Attorney General objected to the taking of testimony as to the constitutionality of this law, on the ground that the court has no authority to take such proof. The objection was thereupon overruled, and the Attorney General excepted." A voluminous mass of evidence was then taken as to the effect of electricity as an agent of death. And upon that evidence it was argued that the punishment in that form was cruel and unusual within the inhibition of the constitutions of the United States and of the State of New York, and that therefore the act in question was unconstitutional.

The county judge observed that the "Constitution of the United States and that of the State of New York, in language almost identical, provide against cruel and inhuman punishment, but it may be remarked, in passing, that with the former we have no present concern, as the prohibition therein contained has no reference to punishments inflicted in state courts for crimes against the State, but is addressed solely to the national government and operates as a restriction on its power." He held that the presumption of constitutionality had not been overcome by the prisoner, because he had not "made it appear by proofs or otherwise, beyond doubt, that the statute of 1888 in regard to the infliction of the death penalty provides a cruel and unusual, and therefore unconstitutional, punishment, and that a force of electricity to kill any human subject with celerity and certainty, when scientifically applied, cannot be generated." He, therefore, made an order dismissing the writ of *habeas corpus*, and remanding the relator to the custody of the respondent. From this order an appeal was taken to the [New York] Supreme Court, which affirmed the judgment of the county judge. . . .

Appeals to Federal Courts

From this judgment of the [New York] Supreme Court an appeal was prosecuted to the [U.S.] Court of Appeals, and the order appealed from was affirmed. It was said for the court by O'Brien, J.: "The only question involved in this appeal is whether this enactment [state law allowing electrocution] is in conflict with the provision of the state constitution which forbids the infliction of cruel and unusual punishment. . . . If it cannot be made to appear that a law is in conflict with the constitution, by argument deduced from the language of the law itself or from matters of which a court can take judicial notice, then the act must stand. The testimony of expert or other witnesses is not admissible to show that in carrying out a law enacted by the legislature some provision of the constitution may possibly be violated." The determination of the legislature that the use of electricity as an agency for producing death constituted a more humane method of executing the judgment of the court in capital cases, was held conclusive. The opinion concludes as follows: "We have examined this testimony and can find but little in it to warrant the belief that this new mode of execution is cruel, within the meaning of the constitution, though it is certainly unusual. On the contrary, we agree with the court below that it removes every reasonable doubt that the application of electricity to the vital parts of the human body, under such conditions and in the manner contemplated by the statute, must result in instantaneous, and consequently in painless, death." At the same term of the Court of Appeals the appeal of the relator from the judgment on the indictment against him was heard, and that judgment affirmed. Among other points made upon that appeal was this, that the sentence imposed was illegal and unconstitutional, as being a cruel and unusual punishment, but the court decided, as in the case of the appeal from the order under consideration here, that the position was untenable, and that the act was not unconstitutional because of the new mode adopted to bring about death. . . .

The New York Statute

It appears that the first step which led to the enactment of the law was a statement contained in the annual message of the governor of the State of New York, transmitted to the legislature January 6, 1885, as follows: "The present mode of executing criminals by hanging has come down to us from the dark ages, and it may well be questioned whether the science of the present day cannot provide a means for taking the life of such as are condemned to die in a less barbarous manner. I commend this suggestion to the consideration of the legislature." The legislature accordingly appointed a commission to investigate and report "the most humane and practical method known to modern science of carrying into effect the sentence of death in capital cases." This commission reported in favor of execution by electricity, and accompanied their report by a bill which was enacted and became chapter 489 of the Laws of 1888. Laws of New York, 1888, 778. Among other changes, section

505 of the Code of Criminal Procedure of New York was amended so as to read as follows: "§ 505. The punishment of death must, in every case, be inflicted by causing to pass through the body of the convict a current of electricity of sufficient intensity to cause death, and the application of such current must be continued until such convict is dead." Various other amendments were made, not necessary to be considered here.

Sections 10, 11 and 12 of the act are as follows:

"§ 10. Nothing contained in any provision of this act applies to a crime committed at any time before the day when this act takes effect. Such crime must be punished according to the provisions of law existing when it is committed, in the same manner as if this act had not been passed; and the provisions of law for the infliction of the penalty of death upon convicted criminals, in existence on the day prior to the passage of this act, are continued in existence and applicable to all crimes punishable by death, which have been or may be committed before the time when this act takes effect. A crime punishable by death committed after the beginning of the day when this act takes effect, must be punished according to the provisions of this act, and not otherwise.

"§ 11. All acts and parts of acts inconsistent with the provisions of this act are hereby repealed.

"§ 12. This act shall take effect on the first day of January, one thousand eight hundred and eighty-nine, and shall apply to all convictions for crimes punishable by death, committed on or after that date."

Kemmler was indicted for and convicted of a murder committed on the 29th day of March, 1889, and therefore came within the statute. . . .

Cruel and Unusual Punishment

Section 5 of article 1, of the constitution of the State of New York, provides that "excessive bail shall not be required, nor excessive fines imposed, nor shall cruel and unusual punishments be inflicted, nor shall witnesses be unreasonably detained." The Eighth Amendment to the Federal Constitution reads thus: "Excessive bail shall not be required, nor excessive fines imposed, nor cruel and unusual punishments inflicted." By the Fourteenth Amendment it is provided that: "All persons born or naturalized in the United States, and subject to the jurisdiction thereof, are citizens of the United States and of the State wherein they reside. No State shall make or enforce any law which shall abridge the privileges or immunities of citizens of the United States; nor shall any State deprive any person of life, liberty or property without due process of law; nor deny to any person within its jurisdiction the equal protection of the laws." It is not contended, as it could not be, that the Eighth Amendment was intended to apply to the States, but it is urged that the provision of the Fourteenth Amendment, which forbids a State to make or enforce any law which shall abridge the privileges or immunities of citizens of the United States, is a prohibition on the State from the imposition of cruel and unusual punishments, and that such punishments are also prohibited by inclusion in the term "due process of law."

The provision in reference to cruel and unusual punishments was taken from the well-known act of Parliament of 1688, entitled "An act declaring the rights and liberties of the subject, and settling the succession of the crown," in which, after rehearsing various grounds of grievance, and among others, that "excessive bail hath been required of Persons committed in criminal cases, to elude the benefit of the laws made for the liberty of the subjects; and excessive fines have been imposed; and illegal and cruel punishments inflicted," it is declared that "excessive bail ought not to be required, nor excessive fines imposed, nor cruel and unusual punishments inflicted."

This Declaration of Rights had reference to the acts of the executive and judicial departments of the government of England; but the language in question as used in the constitution of the State of New York was intended particularly to operate upon the legislature of the State, to whose control the punishment of crime was almost wholly confided. So that, if the punishment prescribed for an offence against the laws of the State were manifestly cruel and unusual, as burning at the stake, crucifixion, breaking on the wheel, or the like, it would be the duty of the courts to adjudge such penalties to be within the constitutional prohibition. And we think this equally true of the Eighth Amendment, in its application to Congress.

In *Wilkerson v. Utah* [1878], Mr. Justice Clifford, in delivering the opinion of the court, referring to [lawyer William] Blackstone, said: "Difficulty would attend the effort to define with exactness the extent of the constitutional provision, which provides that cruel and unusual punishments shall not be inflicted; but it is safe to affirm that punishments of torture, such as those mentioned by the commentator referred to, and all others in the same line of unnecessary cruelty, are forbidden by that amendment to the Constitution." Punishments are cruel when they involve torture or a lingering death; but the punishment of death is not cruel, within the meaning of that word as used in the Constitution. It implies there something inhuman and barbarous, something more than the mere extinguishment of life.

The Role of the State Legislature

The courts of New York held that the mode adopted in this instance might be said to be unusual because it was new, but that it could not be assumed to be cruel in the light of that common knowledge which has stamped certain punishments as such; that it was for the legislature to say in what manner sentence of death should be executed; that this act was passed in the effort to devise a more humane method of reaching the result; that the courts were bound to presume that the legislature was possessed of the facts upon which it took action. . . .

The decision of the state courts sustaining the validity

of the act under the state constitution is not reëxaminable here, nor was that decision against any title, right, privilege, or immunity specially set up or claimed by the petitioner under the Constitution of the United States.

Treating it as involving an adjudication that the statute was not repugnant to the Federal Constitution, that conclusion was so plainly right that we should not be justified in allowing the writ upon the ground that error might have supervened therein. . . .

In order to reverse the judgment of the highest court of the State of New York, we should be compelled to hold that it had committed an error so gross as to amount in law to a denial by the State of due process of law to one accused of crime, or of some right secured to him by the Constitution of the United States. We have no hesitation in saying that this we cannot do upon the record before us.

The application for a writ of error is *Denied.*

The Death Penalty Is Not as Cruel and Unusual as Life Imprisonment

JACQUES BARZUN

The following article was written a decade before the landmark 1972 case of Furman v. Georgia, *in which the U.S. Supreme Court ruled that the death penalty was cruel and unusual punishment. Without using the constitutionally based term "cruel and unusual punishment," the author, social historian Jacques Barzun, supports his pro-death-penalty stance by describing what he sees as the barbarism and indignities of an option much worse than the sentence of death: life imprisonment. Born in France in 1907, Barzun came to the United States after World War I and began his studies of law and history at Columbia University in 1920. He remained at Columbia for his entire professional career, serving as dean of faculties, provost, and professor of history. Barzun is the author of thirty books, including the best sellers* The Teacher in America *(1945),* The House of Intellect *(1959), and* From Dawn to Decadence: 500 Years of Western Cultural Life, 1500 to the Present *(2000).*

I readily concede at the outset that present ways of dealing out capital punishment are as revolting as Mr. [Arthur]

Jacques Barzun, "In Favor of Capital Punishment," *The American Scholar*, Spring 1962, pp. 181–91. Copyright © 1962, renewed 1990 by Jacques Barzun. Reproduced by permission of the publishers.

Koestler says in his harrowing volume, *Hanged by the Neck* (1961). Like many of our prisons, our modes of execution should change. But this objection to barbarity does not mean that capital punishment—or rather, judicial homicide—should not go on. . . .

As in all great questions, the moralist must choose, and choosing has a price. I happen to think that if a person of adult body has not been endowed with adequate controls against irrationally taking the life of another, that person must be judicially, painlessly, regretfully killed before that mindless body's horrible automation repeats.

Appropriate Punishment

I say "irrationally" taking life, because it is often possible to feel great sympathy with a murderer. Certain *crimes passionnels* [crimes of passion] can be forgiven without being condoned. Blackmailers invite direct retribution. Long provocation can be an excuse, as in that engaging case of some years ago, in which a respectable carpenter of seventy found he could no longer stand the incessant nagging of his wife. While she excoriated him from her throne in the kitchen—a daily exercise for fifty years—the husband went to his bench and came back with a hammer in each hand to settle the score. The testimony to his character, coupled with the sincerity implied by the two hammers, was enough to have him sent into quiet and brief seclusion.

But what are we to say of the type of motive disclosed in a journal published by the inmates of one of our Federal penitentiaries? The author is a bank robber who confesses that money is not his object:

> My mania for power, socially, sexually, and otherwise can feel no degree of satisfaction until I feel sure I have struck the ultimate of submission and terror in the minds and bodies of my victims. . . . It's very difficult to explain all the queer fascinating sensations pounding and surging through me while I'm holding a gun on a victim, watching his body tremble and sweat. . . . This is the

moment when all the rationalized hypocrisies of civilization are suddenly swept away and two men stand there facing each other morally and ethically naked, and right and wrong are the absolute commands of the man behind the gun.

This confused echo of modern literature and modern science defines the choice before us. Anything deserving the name of cure for such a man presupposes not only a laborious individual psychoanalysis, with the means to conduct and to sustain it, socially and economically, but also a re-education of the mind, so as to throw into correct perspective the garbled ideas of Freud and Nietzsche, Gide and Dostoevski, which this power-seeker and his fellows have derived from the culture and temper of our times. Ideas are tenacious and give continuity to emotion. Failing a second birth of heart and mind, we must ask: How soon will this sufferer sacrifice a bank clerk in the interests of making civilization less hypocritical? And we must certainly question the wisdom of affording him more than one chance. The abolitionists' advocacy of an unconditional "let live" is in truth part of the same cultural tendency that animates the killer. The Western peoples' revulsion from power in domestic and foreign policy has made of the state a sort of counterpart of the bank robber: both having power and neither knowing how to use it. Both waste lives because hypnotized by irrelevant ideas and crippled by contradictory emotions. If psychiatry were sure of its ground in diagnosing the individual case, a philosopher might consider whether such dangerous obsessions should not be guarded against by judicial homicide *before* the shooting starts.

I raise the question not indeed to recommend the prophylactic execution of potential murderers, but to introduce the last two perplexities that the abolitionists dwarf or obscure by their concentration on changing an isolated penalty. One of these is the scale by which to judge the offenses society wants to repress. I can for example imagine a truly democratic state in which it would be deemed a form of treason punishable by death to create a disturbance in any court or deliberative assembly. The aim would be to recognize the sanctity of orderly discourse in arriving at justice, assessing criticism and defining policy. Under such a law, a natural selection would operate to remove permanently from the scene persons who, let us say, neglect argument in favor of banging on the desk with their shoe. Similarly, a bullying minority in a diet, parliament or skupshtina would be prosecuted for treason to the most sacred institutions when fists or flying inkwells replace rhetoric. That the mere suggestion of such a law sounds ludicrous shows how remote we are from civilized institutions, and hence how gradual should be our departure from the severity of judicial homicide.

The Barbarity of Imprisonment

I say gradual and I do not mean standing still. For there is one form of barbarity in our law that I want to see mitigated before any other. I mean imprisonment. The enemies of capital punishment—and liberals generally—seem to be satisfied with any legal outcome so long as they themselves avoid the vicarious guilt of shedding blood. They speak of the sanctity of life, but have no concern with its quality. They give no impression of ever having read what it is certain they have read, from [Oscar] Wilde's *De Profundis* to the latest account of prison life by a convicted homosexual. Despite the infamy of concentration camps, despite Mr. Charles Burney's remarkable work, *Solitary Confinement*, despite riots in prisons, despite the round of escape, recapture and return in chains, the abolitionists' imagination tells them nothing about the reality of being caged. They read without a qualm, indeed they read with rejoicing, the hideous irony of "Killer Gets Life"; they sigh with relief instead of horror. They do not see and suffer the cell, the drill, the clothes, the stench, the food; they do not feel the sexual racking of young and old bodies, the hateful promiscuity, the insane monotony, the mass degradation, the impotent hatred. They do not remember from [Italian writer] Silvio Pellico that only a strong political faith, with a hope of final victory, can steel a man to endure long detention. They forget that Joan of Arc, when offered "life," preferred burning at the stake. Quite of another mind, the abolitionists point with pride to the "model prisoners" that murderers often turn out to be. As if a model prisoner were not, first, a contradiction in terms, and second, an exemplar of what a free society should not want.

I said a moment ago that the happy advocates of the life sentence appear not to have understood what we know they have read. No more do they appear to read what they themselves write. In the preface to his useful volume of cases, *Hanged in Error*, Mr. Leslie Hale, M.P., refers to the tardy recognition of a minor miscarriage of justice—one year in jail: "The prisoner emerged to find that his wife had died and that his children and his aged parents had been removed to the workhouse. By the time a small payment had been assessed as 'compensation' the victim was incurably insane." So far we are as indignant with the law as Mr. Hale. But what comes next? He cites the famous Evans case, in which it is very probable that the wrong man was hanged, and he exclaims: "While such mistakes are possible, should society impose an irrevocable sentence?" Does Mr. Hale really ask us to believe that the sentence passed on the first man, whose wife died and who went insane, was in any sense *revocable?* Would not any man rather be Evans dead than that other wretch "emerging" with his small compensation and his reasons for living gone?

Nothing is revocable here below, imprisonment least of all. The agony of a trial itself is punishment, and acquittal wipes out nothing. Read the heart-rending diary of William Wallace, accused quite implausibly of having murdered his wife and "saved" by the Court of Criminal Appeals—but saved for what? Brutish ostracism by everyone and a few years of solitary despair. The cases of Adolf Beck, of Oscar Slater, of the unhappy Brooklyn bank teller who vaguely resembled a forger and spent eight years in Sing Sing only to "emerge" a broken, friendless, useless, "compensated" man—all these, if the dignity of the individual has any meaning, had better have been dead before the prison door ever opened for them. This is what counsel always says to the jury in the course of a murder trial and counsel is right: far better hang this man than "give him life." For my part, I would choose death without hesitation. If that option is abolished, a demand will one day be heard to claim it as a privilege in the name of human dignity. I shall believe in the abolitionist's present views only after he has emerged from twelve months in a convict cell.

Imprisonment Is Worse than Death

The detached observer may want to interrupt here and say that the argument has now passed from reasoning to emotional preference. Whereas the objector to capital punishment *feels* that death is the greatest of evils, I *feel* that imprisonment is worse than death. A moment's thought will show that feeling is the appropriate arbiter. All reasoning about what is right, civilized and moral rests upon sentiment, like mathematics. Only, in trying to persuade others, it is important to single out the fundamental feeling, the prime intuition, and from it to reason justly. In my view, to profess respect for human life and be willing to see it spent in a penitentiary is to entertain liberal feelings frivolously. To oppose the death penalty because, unlike a prison term, it is irrevocable is to argue fallaciously.

In the propaganda for abolishing the death sentence the recital of numerous miscarriages of justice commits the same error and implies the same callousness: what is at fault in our present system is not the sentence but the fallible procedure. Capital cases being one in a thousand or more, who can be cheerful at the thought of all the "revocable" errors? What the miscarriages point to is the need for reforming the jury system, the rules of evidence, the customs of prosecution, the machinery of appeal. The failure to see that this is the great task reflects the sentimentality I spoke of earlier, that which responds chiefly to the excitement of the unusual. A writer on death and the Supreme Court is at pains to point out that when that tribunal reviews a capital case, the judges are particularly anxious and careful. What a left-handed compliment to the highest judicial conscience of the country! Fortunately, some of the champions of the misjudged see the issue more clearly. Many of those who are thought wrongly convicted now languish in jail because the jury was uncertain or because a doubting governor commuted the death sentence. Thus Dr. Samuel H. Sheppard, Jr., convicted of his wife's murder in the second degree is serving a sentence that is supposed to run for the term of his natural life. The story of his numerous trials, as told by Mr. Paul Holmes, suggests that police incompetence, newspaper demagogy, public envy of affluence and the mischances of legal procedure fashioned the result. But Dr. Sheppard's vindicator is under no illusion as to the conditions that this "lucky" evader of the electric chair will face if he is granted parole after ten years: "It will carry with it no right to resume his life as a physician. His privilege to practice medicine was blotted out with his conviction. He must all his life bear the stigma of a parolee, subject to unceremonious return to confinement for life for the slightest misstep. More than this, he must live out his life as a convicted murderer."

Questions of Moral Conscience

What does the moral conscience of today think it is doing? If such a man is a dangerous repeater of violent acts, what right has the state to let him loose after ten years? What is, in fact, the meaning of a "life sentence" that peters out long before life? Paroling looks suspiciously like an expression of social remorse for the pain of incarceration, coupled with a wish to avoid "unfavorable publicity" by freeing a suspect. The man is let out when the fuss has died down; which would mean that he was not under lock and key for our protection at all. He *was* being punished, just a little—for so prison seems in the abolitionist's distorted view, and in the jury's and the prosecutor's, whose "second-degree" murder suggests killing someone "just a little."

If, on the other hand, execution and life imprisonment are judged too severe and the accused is expected to be harmless hereafter—punishment being ruled out as illiberal—what has society gained by wrecking his life and damaging that of his family?

What we accept, and what the abolitionist will clamp upon us all the more firmly if he succeeds, is an incoherence which is not remedied by the belief that second-degree murder merits a kind of second-degree death; that a doubt as to the identity of a killer is resolved by commuting real death into intolerable life; and that our ignorance whether a maniac will strike again can be hedged against by measuring "good behavior" within the gates and then releasing the subject upon the public in the true spirit of experimentation.

These are some of the thoughts I find I cannot escape when I read and reflect upon this grave subject. If, as I think, they are relevant to any discussion of change and reform, resting as they do on the direct and concrete perception of what happens, then the simple meliorists who expect to breathe a purer air by abolishing the death penalty are deceiving themselves and us. The issue is for the public to judge; but I for one shall not sleep easier for knowing that in England and America and the West generally a hundred more human beings are kept alive in degrading conditions to face a hopeless future; while others—possibly less conscious, certainly less controlled—benefit from a premature freedom dangerous alike to themselves and society. In short, I derive no comfort from the illusion that in giving up one manifest protection of the law-abiding, we who might well be in any of these three roles—victim, prisoner, licensed killer—have struck a blow for the sanctity of human life.

The Death Penalty Is Cruel and Unusual Punishment

WILLIAM O. DOUGLAS AND WILLIAM J. BRENNAN JR.

In 1972 the case of Furman v. Georgia *was argued before the U.S. Supreme Court. William Furman, an African American, was convicted of the murder of a white man in the state of Georgia and sentenced to die. (The cases of two other African American males were also included in this same suit. They were convicted of raping white victims and were also sentenced to die.) The Georgia law under which Furman was convicted allowed a jury to impose the death penalty for capital (murder) cases. His sentence was appealed to the U.S. Supreme Court on the grounds that giving a jury such wide discretion to invoke the death penalty violated the Eighth Amendment's cruel and unusual punishment clause. For the first time in the history of American jurisprudence, the Supreme Court held that "the imposition and carrying out of the death penalty . . . constitute cruel and unusual punishment." However, the Supreme Court did not speak with one majority voice. Although five of the nine justices believed that it was wrong to impose the death penalty under the Georgia laws that were used to convict the three defendants, each of the five had different reasons for arriving at that conclusion. After issuing their brief summary opinion, each of the five majority justices composed a separate concurring opinion. Excerpts from the opinions of Justices Douglas and Brennan*

William O. Douglas and William J. Brennan Jr., opinions, *Furman v. Georgia*, U.S. Supreme Court, 1972.

are included here. Justice Douglas writes the death penalty is cruel and unusual because of the likelihood that judges and juries discriminate against poor or minority defendants. Justice Brennan concludes that because punishment by death is extremely severe, administered arbitrarily, and unacceptable to many in society, it represents cruel and unusual punishment and is therefore unconstitutional. William O. Douglas served as an associate justice from 1939 to 1975. William J. Brennan Jr. served as an associate justice from 1956 to 1990.

Petitioner in No. 69-5003 was convicted of murder in Georgia and was sentenced to death. . . . Petitioner in No. 69-5030 was convicted of rape in Georgia and was sentenced to death. . . . Petitioner in No. 69-5031 was convicted of rape in Texas and was sentenced to death. . . . Certiorari [a request that records from a lower court be transferred to a higher court] was granted limited to the following question: "Does the imposition and carrying out of the death penalty in (these cases) constitute cruel and unusual punishment in violation of the Eighth and Fourteenth Amendments?" The Court holds that the imposition and carrying out of the death penalty in these cases constitute cruel and unusual punishment in violation of the Eighth and Fourteenth Amendments. The judgment in each case is therefore reversed insofar as it leaves undisturbed the death sentence imposed, and the cases are remanded for further proceedings.

Concurring Opinion of Justice Douglas

The generality of a law inflicting capital punishment is one thing. What may be said of the validity of a law on the books and what may be done with the law in its application do, or may, lead to quite different conclusions. It would seem to be incontestable that the death penalty inflicted on one defendant is "unusual" if it discriminates against him by reason of his race, religion, wealth, social position, or class, or if it is imposed under a procedure that gives room for the play of such prejudices. . . .

The words "cruel and unusual" certainly include penalties that are barbaric. But the words, at least when read in light of the English proscription against selective and irregular use of penalties, suggest that it is "cruel and unusual" to apply the death penalty—or any other penalty—selectively to minorities whose numbers are few, who are outcasts of society, and who are unpopular, but whom society is willing to see suffer though it would not countenance general application of the same penalty across the board. . . .

There is increasing recognition of the fact that the basic theme of equal protection is implicit in "cruel and unusual" punishments. "A penalty . . . should be considered 'unusually' imposed if it is administered arbitrarily or discriminatorily.". . .

We cannot say from facts disclosed in these records that these defendants were sentenced to death because they were black. Yet our task is not restricted to an effort to divine what motives impelled these death penalties. Rather, we deal with a system of law and of justice that leaves to the uncontrolled discretion of judges or juries the determination whether defendants committing these crimes should die or be imprisoned. Under these laws no standards govern the selection of the penalty. People live or die, dependent on the whim of 1 man or of 12. . . .

Laws Must Be Nonselective and Nonarbitrary

In a Nation committed to equal protection of the laws there is no permissible "caste" aspect of law enforcement. Yet we know that the discretion of judges and juries in imposing the death penalty enables the penalty to be selectively applied, feeding prejudices against the accused if he is poor and despised, and lacking political clout, or if he is a member of a suspect or unpopular minority, and saving those who by social position may be in a more protected position. In ancient Hindu law a Brahman was exempt from capital punishment, and under that law, "generally, in the law books, punishment increased in severity as social status diminished." We have, I fear, taken in practice the same position, partially as a result of making the death penalty discretionary and partially as a result of the ability of the rich to purchase the services of the most respected and most resourceful legal talent in the Nation.

The high service rendered by the "cruel and unusual" punishment clause of the Eighth Amendment is to require legislatures to write penal laws that are evenhanded, nonselective, and nonarbitrary, and to require judges to see to it that general laws are not applied sparsely, selectively, and spottily to unpopular groups.

A law that stated that anyone making more than $50,000 would be exempt from the death penalty would plainly fall, as would a law that in terms said that blacks, those who never went beyond the fifth grade in school, those who made less than $3,000 a year, or those who were unpopular or unstable should be the only people executed. A law which in the overall view reaches that result in practice has no more sanctity than a law which in terms provides the same.

Thus, these discretionary statutes are unconstitutional in their operation. They are pregnant with discrimination and discrimination is an ingredient not compatible with the idea of equal protection of the laws that is implicit in the ban on "cruel and unusual" punishments. . . .

Concurring Opinion of Justice Brennan

There are, then, four principles by which we may determine whether a particular punishment is "cruel and unusual.". . . If a punishment is unusually severe, if there is a strong probability that it is inflicted arbitrarily, if it is substantially rejected by contemporary society, and if there is no reason to believe that it serves any penal purpose more effectively than some less severe punishment then the continued infliction of that punishment violates the command of the Clause that the State may not inflict inhuman and uncivilized punishments upon those convicted of crimes. . . .

The question, then, is whether the deliberate infliction of death is today consistent with the command of the Clause that the State may not inflict punishments that do not comport with human dignity. I will analyze the punishment of death in terms of the principles set out above and the cumulative test to which they lead: It is a denial of human dignity for the State arbitrarily to subject a person to an unusually severe punishment that society has indicated it does not regard as acceptable, and that cannot be shown to serve any penal purpose more effectively than a significantly less drastic punishment. Under these principles and this test, death is today a "cruel and unusual" punishment.

Death Penalty in the United States

Death is a unique punishment in the United States. In a society that so strongly affirms the sanctity of life, not surprisingly the common view is that death is the ultimate sanction. This natural human feeling appears all about us. There has been no national debate about punishment, in general or by imprisonment, comparable to the debate about the punishment of death. No other punishment has been so continuously restricted, nor has any State yet abolished prisons, as some have abolished this punishment. And those States that still inflict death reserve it for the most heinous crimes. Juries, of course, have always treated death cases differently, as have governors exercising their commutation powers. Criminal defendants are of the same view. . . . Some legislatures have required particular procedures, such as two-stage trials and automatic appeals, applicable only in death cases. . . . This Court, too, almost always treats death cases as a class apart. And the unfortunate effect of this punishment upon the functioning of the judicial process is well known; no other punishment has a similar effect.

The only explanation for the uniqueness of death is its extreme severity. Death is today an unusually severe punishment, unusual in its pain, in its finality, and in its enormity. No other existing punishment is comparable to death in terms of physical and mental suffering. Although our information is not conclusive, it appears that there is no method available that guarantees an immediate and painless death. Since the discontinuance of flogging as a constitutionally permissible punishment, death remains as the only punishment that may involve the conscious infliction of physical pain. In addition, we know that mental pain is an inseparable part of our practice of punishing criminals by death, for the prospect of pending execution exacts a frightful toll during the inevitable long wait between the imposition of sentence and the actual infliction of death. . . .

The unusual severity of death is manifested most clearly in its finality and enormity. Death, in these respects, is in a class by itself. . . .

Death is truly an awesome punishment. The calculated killing of a human being by the State involves, by its very nature, a denial of the executed person's humanity. The contrast with the plight of a person punished by imprisonment is evident. An individual in prison does not lose "the right to have rights.". . . His punishment is not irrevocable. Apart from the common charge, grounded upon the recognition of human fallibility, that the punishment of death must inevitably be inflicted upon innocent men, we know that death has been the lot of men whose convictions were unconstitutionally secured in view of later, retroactively applied, holdings of this Court. The punishment itself may have been unconstitutionally inflicted, see *Witherspoon v. Illinois*, yet the finality of death precludes relief. . . .

In comparison to all other punishments today, then, the deliberate extinguishment of human life by the State is uniquely degrading to human dignity. I would not hesitate to hold, on that ground alone, that death is today a "cruel and unusual" punishment, were it not that death is a punishment of long-standing usage and acceptance in this country. I therefore turn to the second principle—that the State may not arbitrarily inflict an unusually severe punishment.

The outstanding characteristic of our present practice of punishing criminals by death is the infrequency with which we resort to it. The evidence is conclusive that death is not the ordinary punishment for any crime. There has been a steady decline in the infliction of this punishment in every decade since the 1930's, the earliest period for which accurate statistics are available. In the 1930's, executions averaged 167 per year; in the 1940's, the average was 128; in the 1950's, it was 72; and in the years 1960–1962, it was 48. There have been a total of 46 executions since then, 36 of them in 1963–1964. Yet our population and the number of capital crimes committed have increased greatly over the past four decades. The contemporary rarity of the infliction of this punishment is thus the end result of a long-continued decline. . . .

When a country of over 200 million people inflicts an unusually severe punishment no more than 50 times a year, the inference is strong that the punishment is not being regularly and fairly applied. To dispel it would indeed require a clear showing of nonarbitrary infliction. . . .

Death Penalty Rejected and Restricted

When there is a strong probability that an unusually severe and degrading punishment is being inflicted arbitrarily, we may well expect that society will disapprove of its infliction. I turn, therefore, to the third principle. An examination of the history and present operation of the American practice of punishing criminals by death reveals that this punishment has been almost totally rejected by contemporary society. . . .

From the beginning of our Nation, the punishment of death has stirred acute public controversy. Although pragmatic arguments for and against the punishment have been frequently advanced, this long-standing and heated controversy cannot be explained solely as the result of differences over the practical wisdom of a particular government policy. At bottom, the battle has been waged on moral grounds. The country has debated whether a society for which the dignity of the individual is the supreme value can, without a fundamental inconsistency, follow the practice of deliberately putting some of its members to death. . . .

Our practice of punishing criminals by death has changed greatly over the years. One significant change has been in our methods of inflicting death. Although this country never embraced the more violent and repulsive methods employed in England, we did for a long time rely almost exclusively upon the gallows and the firing squad. Since the development of the supposedly more humane methods of electrocution late in the 19th century and lethal gas in the 20th, however, hanging and shooting have virtually ceased. Our concern for decency and human dignity, moreover, has compelled changes in the circumstances surrounding the execution itself. No longer does our society countenance the spectacle of public executions, once thought desirable as a deterrent to criminal behavior by others. Today we reject public executions as debasing and brutalizing to us all.

Also significant is the drastic decrease in the crimes for which the punishment of death is actually inflicted. While esoteric capital crimes remain on the books. since 1930 murder and rape have accounted for nearly 99 percent of the total executions, and murder alone for about 87 percent. In addition, the crime of capital murder has itself been limited. As the Court noted in *McGautha v. California*, there was in this country a "rebellion against the common-law rule imposing a mandatory death sentence on all convicted murderers.". . . In consequence, virtually all death sentences today are discretionarily imposed. Finally, it is significant that nine States no longer inflict the punishment of death under any circumstances, and five others have restricted it to extremely rare crimes.

Thus, although "the death penalty has been employed throughout our history," *Trop v. Dulles* [1958], in fact the history of this punishment is one of successive restriction. What was once a common punishment has become, in the context of a continuing moral debate, increasingly rare. The evolution of this punishment evidences, not that it is an inevitable part of the American scene, but that it has proved progressively more troublesome to the national conscience. The result of this movement is our current system of administering the punishment, under which death sentences are rarely imposed and death is even more rarely inflicted. . . .

The progressive decline in, and the current rarity of, the infliction of death demonstrate that our society seriously questions the appropriateness of this punishment today. . . .

The final principle to be considered is that an unusually severe and degrading punishment may not be excessive in view of the purposes for which it is inflicted. This principle, too, is related to the others. When there is a strong probability that the State is arbitrarily inflicting an unusually severe punishment that is subject to grave societal doubts, it is likely also that the punishment cannot be shown to be serving any penal purpose that could not be served equally well by some less severe punishment. . . .

In sum, the punishment of death is inconsistent with all four principles: Death is an unusually severe and degrading punishment; there is a strong probability that it is inflicted arbitrarily; its rejection by contemporary society is virtually total; and there is no reason to believe that it serves any penal purpose more effectively than the less severe punishment of imprisonment. The function of these principles is to enable a court to determine whether a punishment comports with human dignity. Death, quite simply, does not.

The Death Penalty Is Not Always Cruel and Unusual Punishment

POTTER STEWART

In 1972 the U.S. Supreme Court made a landmark ruling in the case of Furman v. Georgia *that the death penalty violated the cruel and unusual punishment clause of the Eighth Amendment of the U.S. Constitution. In the years immediately following the ruling, most state legislatures struggled to understand the guidelines created by the Court when it handed down its decision. In Georgia, the death penalty law was rewritten, according to the state legislature's understanding of the* Furman *case, to allow for capital punishment for six crimes: murder, kidnapping for ransom or where the victim is harmed, armed robbery, rape, treason, and aircraft hijacking. If the defendant was found guilty of one of those crimes, the Georgia law required an additional sentencing phase in which both the prosecution and the defense could offer further evidence relative to arguments for or against the imposition of the death penalty. In addition, the law included a statute listing ten aggravating circumstances. A judge or jury had to find that at least one of these aggravating circumstances applied to the defendant's situation before a death sentence could be imposed. The statute also provided for a special appeals process through the various levels of Geor-*

Potter Stewart, opinion, *Gregg v. Georgia*, U.S. Supreme Court, 1976.

gia's state courts once a death penalty had been imposed.

In the 1976 case of Gregg v. Georgia, *the defendant, Troy Gregg, was convicted of murder and armed robbery and sentenced to death under Georgia's revised death penalty statute. Gregg's appeals of that death sentence reached the U.S. Supreme Court. Supreme Court justice Potter Stewart, writing for the court and joined in his opinion by Justices Lewis Powell and John Paul Stevens, upheld the death sentence. Noting the safeguards for the defendant that were contained within the revised Georgia statute, Stewart determined that Gregg's death sentence was not handed down arbitrarily and was therefore not cruel and unusual punishment. The following selection is an extract of his ruling. Justice Potter Stewart served as an associate justice of the Supreme Court from 1958 to 1981.*

The issue in this case is whether the imposition of the sentence of death for the crime of murder under the law of Georgia violates the Eighth and Fourteenth Amendments.

The petitioner, Troy Gregg, was charged with committing armed robbery and murder. In accordance with Georgia procedure in capital cases, the trial was in two stages, a guilt stage and a sentencing stage. The evidence at the guilt trial established that on November 21, 1973, the petitioner and a traveling companion, Floyd Allen, while hitchhiking north in Florida were picked up by Fred Simmons and Bob Moore. Their car broke down, but they continued north after Simmons purchased another vehicle with some of the cash he was carrying.

While still in Florida, they picked up another hitchhiker, Dennis Weaver, who rode with them to Atlanta, where he was let out about 11 P.M. A short time later the four men interrupted their journey for a rest stop along the highway. The next morning the bodies of Simmons and Moore were discovered in a ditch nearby. . . . The jury found the petitioner guilty of two counts of armed robbery and two counts of murder.

At the penalty stage, which took place before the same jury, neither the prosecutor nor the petitioner's lawyer offered any additional evidence. Both counsel, however, made lengthy arguments dealing generally with the propriety of capital punishment under the circumstances and with the weight of the evidence of guilt. The trial judge instructed the jury that it could recommend either a death sentence or a life prison sentence on each count. The judge further charged the jury that in determining what sentence was appropriate the jury was free to consider the facts and circumstances, if any, presented by the parties in mitigation or aggravation.

Finally, the judge instructed the jury that it "would not be authorized to consider [imposing] the penalty of death" unless it first found beyond a reasonable doubt one of these aggravating circumstances:

> (1) That the offense of murder was committed while the offender was engaged in the commission of two other capital felonies, to-wit the armed robbery of [Simmons and Moore].
>
> (2) That the offender committed the offense of murder for the purpose of receiving money and the automobile described in the indictment.
>
> (3) The offense of murder was outrageously and wantonly vile, horrible and inhuman, in that they [sic] involved the depravity of [the] mind of the defendant.

Finding the first and second of these circumstances, the jury returned verdicts of death on each count.

The Supreme Court of Georgia affirmed the convictions and the imposition of the death sentences for murder.

The Georgia Death Penalty Statute

Before considering the issues presented it is necessary to understand the Georgia statutory scheme for the imposition of the death penalty. The Georgia statute, as amended after our decision in *Furman v. Georgia*, retains the death penalty for six categories of crime: murder, kidnapping for ransom or where the victim is harmed, armed robbery, rape, treason, and aircraft hijacking. The capital defendant's guilt or innocence is determined in the traditional manner, either by a trial judge or a jury, in the first stage of a bifurcated trial. . . . After a verdict, finding, or plea of guilty to a capital crime, a presentence hearing is conducted before whoever made the determination of guilt. The sentencing procedures are essentially the same in both bench and jury trials. At the hearing:

> The judge [or jury] shall hear additional evidence in extenuation, mitigation, and aggravation of punishment, including the record of any prior criminal convictions and pleas of guilty or pleas of nolo contendere [neither admitting nor denying guilt] of the defendant, or the absence of any prior conviction and pleas: Provided, however, that only such evidence in aggravation as the State has made known to the defendant prior to his trial shall be admissible. The judge [or jury] shall also hear argument by the defendant or his counsel and the prosecuting attorney . . . regarding the punishment to be imposed.

The defendant is accorded substantial latitude as to the types of evidence that he may introduce. Evidence considered during the guilt stage may be considered during the sentencing stage without being resubmitted. In the assessment of the appropriate sentence to be imposed the judge is also required to consider or to include in his instructions to the jury "any mitigating circumstances or aggravating circumstances otherwise authorized by law and any of [10] statutory aggravating circumstances which may be supported by the evidence. . . ." The scope of the nonstatutory aggravating or mitigating circumstances is not delineated in the statute. Before a convicted defendant may be sentenced to death, however, except in cases of treason or aircraft hijacking, the jury, or the trial judge in cases tried without a jury, must find beyond a reasonable doubt one of the 10 aggravating circumstances specified in the statute. The sentence of death may be imposed only if the jury (or judge) finds one of the statutory aggravating circumstances and then elects to impose that sentence. If the verdict is death, the jury or judge must specify the aggravating circumstance(s) found. In jury cases, the trial judge is bound by the jury's recommended sentence.

In addition to the conventional appellate process available in all criminal cases, provision is made for special expedited direct review by the Supreme Court of Georgia of the appropriateness of imposing the sentence of death in the particular case. The court is directed to consider "the punishment as well as any errors enumerated by way of appeal," and to determine:

> (1) Whether the sentence of death was imposed under the influence of passion, prejudice, or any arbitrary factor, and

> (2) Whether, in cases other than treason or aircraft hijacking, the evidence supports the jury's or judge's finding of a statutory aggravating circumstance . . . , and

> (3) Whether the sentence of death is excessive or disproportionate to the penalty imposed in similar cases, considering both the crime and the defendant.

If the court affirms a death sentence, it is required to include in its decision reference to similar cases that it has taken into consideration. A transcript and complete record of the trial, as well as a separate report by the trial judge, are transmitted to the court for its use in reviewing the sentence. The report is in the form of a 6½-page questionnaire, designed to elicit information about the defendant, the crime, and the circumstances of the trial. It requires the trial judge to characterize the trial in several ways designed to test for arbitrariness and disproportionality of sentence. Included in the report are responses to detailed questions concerning the quality of the defendant's representation, whether race played a role in the trial, and, whether, in the trial court's judgment, there was any doubt about the defendant's guilt or the appropriateness of the sentence. A copy of the report is served upon defense counsel. Under its special review authority, the court may either affirm the death sentence or remand the case for re-sentencing. In cases in which the death sentence is affirmed there remains the possibility of executive clemency.

Is the Death Penalty Always "Cruel and Unusual"?

We address initially the basic contention that the punishment of death for the crime of murder is, under all circumstances, "cruel and unusual" in violation of the Eighth and Fourteenth Amendments of the Constitution. . . .

The petitioners in the capital cases before the Court today [1976] renew the "standards of decency" [the change over time of society's notion of acceptable behavior] argument, but developments during the four years since *Furman* have undercut substantially the assumptions upon which their argument rested. Despite the continuing debate, dating back to the 19th century, over the morality and utility of capital punishment, it is now evident that a large proportion of American society continues to regard it as an appropriate and necessary criminal sanction.

The most marked indication of society's endorsement of the death penalty for murder is the legislative response to *Furman*. The legislatures of at least 35 States have enacted new statutes that provide for the death penalty for at least some crimes that result in the death of another person. And the Congress of the United States, in 1974, enacted a statute providing the death penalty for aircraft piracy that results in death. These recently adopted statutes have attempted to address the concerns expressed by the Court in *Furman* primarily (i) by specifying the factors to be weighed and the procedures to be followed in deciding when to impose a capital sentence, or (ii) by making the death penalty mandatory for specified crimes. But all of the post-*Furman* statutes make clear that capital punishment itself has not been rejected by the elected representatives of the people. . . .

The jury also is a significant and reliable objective index of contemporary values because it is so directly involved. . . . The Court has said that "one of the most important functions any jury can perform in making . . . a selection [between life imprisonment and death for a defendant convicted in a capital case] is to maintain a link between contemporary community values and the penal system." *Witherspoon v. Illinois* (1968). It may be true that evolving standards have influenced juries in recent decades to be more discriminating in imposing the sentence of death. But the relative infrequency of jury verdicts imposing the death sentence does not indicate rejection of capital punishment *per se*. Rather, the reluctance of juries in many cases to impose the sentence may well reflect the humane feeling that this most irrevocable of sanctions should be reserved for a small number of extreme cases. . . . Indeed, the actions of juries in many States since *Furman* are fully compatible with the legislative judgments, reflected in the new statutes, as to the continued utility and necessity of capital punishment in appropriate cases. At the close of 1974 at least 254 persons had been sentenced to death since *Furman*, and by the end of March 1976, more than 460 persons were subject to death sentences.

As we have seen, however, the Eighth Amendment demands more than that a challenged punishment be acceptable to contemporary society. The Court also must ask whether it comports with the basic concept of human dignity at the core of the Amendment. Although we cannot "invalidate a category of penalties because we deem less severe penalties adequate to serve the ends of penology," *Furman v. Georgia*, the sanction imposed cannot be so totally without penological justification that it results in the gratuitous infliction of suffering.

Purposes of the Death Penalty

The death penalty is said to serve two principal social purposes: retribution and deterrence of capital crimes by prospective offenders. In part, capital punishment is an expression of society's moral outrage at particularly offensive conduct. This function may be unappealing to many, but it is essential in an ordered society that asks its citizens to rely on legal processes rather than self-help to vindicate their wrongs.

> The instinct for retribution is part of the nature of man, and channeling that instinct in the administration of criminal justice serves an important purpose in promoting the stability of a society governed by law. When people begin to believe that organized society is unwilling or unable to impose upon criminal offenders the punishment they "deserve," then there are sown the seeds of anarchy of self-help, vigilante justice, and lynch law. *Furman v. Georgia* (1972).

"Retribution is no longer the dominant objective of the criminal law," *Williams v. New York*, 337 U.S. 241, 248 (1949), but neither is it a forbidden objective nor one inconsistent with our respect for the dignity of men. . . . Indeed, the decision that capital punishment may be the appropriate sanction in extreme cases is an expression of the community's belief that certain crimes are themselves so grievous an affront to humanity that the only adequate response may be the penalty of death. . . .

Although some of the studies suggest that the death penalty may not function as a significantly greater deterrent than lesser penalties, there is no convincing empirical evidence either supporting or refuting this view. We may nevertheless assume safely that there are murderers, such as those who act in passion, for whom the threat of death has little or no deterrent effect. But for many others, the death penalty undoubtedly is a significant deterrent. There are carefully contemplated murders, such as murder for hire, where the possible penalty of death may well enter into the cold calculus that precedes the decision to act. And there are some categories of murder, such as murder by a life prisoner, where other sanctions may not be adequate.

The value of capital punishment as a deterrent of crime is a complex factual issue the resolution of which properly rests with the legislatures, which can evaluate the results of statistical studies in terms of their own local conditions and with a flexibility of approach that is not available to the courts. . . . Indeed, many of the post-*Furman* statutes reflect just such a responsible effort to define those crimes and those criminals for which capital punishment is most probably an effective deterrent.

In sum, we cannot say that the judgment of the Georgia Legislature that capital punishment may be necessary in some cases is clearly wrong. Considerations of federalism, as well as respect for the ability of a legislature to evaluate, in terms of its particular State, the moral consensus concerning the death penalty and its social utility as a sanction, require us to conclude, in the absence of more convincing evidence, that the infliction of death as a punishment for murder is not without justification and thus is not unconstitutionally severe.

Finally, we must consider whether the punishment of death is disproportionate in relation to the crime for which it is imposed. There is no question that death as a punishment is unique in its severity and irrevocability. . . . When a defendant's life is at stake, the Court has been particularly sensitive to insure that every safeguard is observed. . . . But we are concerned here only with the imposition of capital punishment for the crime of murder, and when a life has been taken deliberately by the offender, we cannot say that the punishment is invariably disproportionate to the crime. It is an extreme sanction, suitable to the most extreme of crimes.

We hold that the death penalty is not a form of punishment that may never be imposed, regardless of the circumstances of the offense, regardless of the character of the offender, and regardless of the procedure followed in reaching the decision to impose it. . . .

Analyzing the *Furman* Case

While *Furman* did not hold that the infliction of the death penalty *per se* violates the Constitution's ban on cruel and unusual punishments, it did recognize that the penalty of death is different in kind from any other punishment imposed under our system of criminal justice. Because of the uniqueness of the death penalty, *Furman* held that it could not be imposed under sentencing procedures that created a substantial risk that it would be inflicted in an arbitrary and capricious manner. . . . *Furman* mandates that where discretion is afforded a sentencing body on a matter so grave as the determination of whether a human life should be taken or spared, that discretion must be suitably directed and limited so as to minimize the risk of wholly arbitrary and capricious action. . . .

Jury sentencing has been considered desirable in capital cases in order "to maintain a link between contemporary community values and the penal system—a link without which the determination of punishment could hardly reflect 'the evolving standards of decency that mark the progress of a maturing society.'" But it creates special problems. Much of the information that is relevant to the sentencing decision may have no relevance to the question of guilt, or may even be extremely prejudicial to a fair determination of that question. This problem, however, is scarcely insurmountable. Those who have studied the question suggest that a bifurcated procedure—one in which the question of sentence is not considered until the determination of guilt has been made—is the best answer. . . . When a human life is at stake and when the jury must have information prejudicial to the question of guilt but relevant to the question of penalty in order to impose a rational sentence, a bifurcated system is more likely to ensure elimination of the constitutional deficiencies identified in *Furman*.

But the provision of relevant information under fair procedural rules is not alone sufficient to guarantee that the information will be properly used in the imposition of punishment, especially if sentencing is performed by a jury. Since the members of a jury will have had little, if any, previous experience in sentencing, they are unlikely to be skilled in dealing with the information they are given. . . . To the extent that this problem is inherent in jury sentencing, it may not be totally correctable. It seems clear, however, that the problem will be alleviated if the jury is given guidance regarding the factors about the crime and the defendant that the State, representing organized society, deems particularly relevant to the sentencing decision. . . .

In summary, the concerns expressed in *Furman* that the penalty of death not be imposed in an arbitrary or capricious manner can be met by a carefully drafted statute that ensures that the sentencing authority is given adequate information and guidance. As a general proposition these concerns are best met by a system that provides for a bifurcated proceeding at which the sentencing authority is apprised of the information relevant to the imposition of sentence and provided with standards to guide its use of the information. . . .

Georgia's Revised Sentencing Procedures

The basic concern of *Furman* centered on those defendants who were being condemned to death capriciously and arbitrarily. Under the procedures before the Court in that case, sentencing authorities were not directed to give attention to the nature or circumstances of the crime committed or to the character or record of the defendant. Left unguided, juries imposed the death sentence in a way that could only be called freakish. The new Georgia sentencing procedures, by contrast, focus the jury's attention on the particularized nature of the crime and the particularized characteristics of the individual defendant. While the jury is permitted to consider any aggravating or mitigating circumstances, it must find and identify at least one statutory aggravating factor before it may impose a penalty of death. In this way the jury's discretion is channeled. No longer can a jury wantonly and freakishly impose the death sentence; it is always circumscribed by the legislative guidelines. In addition, the review function of the Supreme Court of Georgia affords additional assurance that the concerns that prompted our decision in *Furman* are not present to any significant degree in the Georgia procedure applied here.

For the reasons expressed in this opinion, we hold that the statutory system under which Gregg was sentenced to death does not violate the Constitution. Accordingly, the judgment of the Georgia Supreme Court is affirmed. It is so ordered.

Executing Juveniles Is Cruel and Unusual Punishment

JOHN PAUL STEVENS

In the early 1980s William Thompson was convicted of brutally murdering his brother-in-law. At the time of the murder, Thompson had been fifteen years old, but he was ordered to stand trial as an adult and was sentenced to death. Thompson appealed his case to the U.S. Supreme Court. In an opinion rendered in 1988, Justice John Paul Stevens ruled that imposing the death penalty for an offense committed by someone younger than sixteen amounts to cruel and unusual punishment and is therefore unconstitutional. In arriving at his finding, Stevens considered legislative minimum age laws, the opinions of professional law organizations about the execution of juveniles, and the possibility of any societal good resulting from applying the death penalty to juveniles. John Paul Stevens was appointed to the U.S. Supreme Court in 1975 by President Gerald Ford.

Because there is no claim that the punishment [of death] would be excessive if the crime had been committed by an adult, only a brief statement of facts is necessary. In concert with three older persons, petitioner [defendant accused of crime] actively participated in the brutal murder of his former brother-in-law in the early morning hours of January 23, 1983. The evidence disclosed that the victim

John Paul Stevens, opinion, *Thompson v. Oklahoma*, U.S. Supreme Court, 1988.

had been shot twice, and that his throat, chest, and abdomen had been cut. He also had multiple bruises and a broken leg. His body had been chained to a concrete block and thrown into a river where it remained for almost four weeks. Each of the four participants was tried separately and each was sentenced to death.

Because petitioner was a "child" as a matter of Oklahoma law, the District Attorney filed a statutory petition, seeking an order finding "that said child is competent and had the mental capacity to know and appreciate the wrongfulness of his [conduct]." After a hearing, the trial court concluded "that there are virtually no *reasonable* prospects for rehabilitation of William Wayne Thompson within the juvenile system and that William Wayne Thompson should be held accountable for his acts as if he were an adult and should be certified to stand trial as an adult.". . .

At the penalty phase of the trial, the prosecutor asked the jury to find two aggravating circumstances: that the murder was especially heinous, atrocious, or cruel; and that there was a probability that the defendant would commit criminal acts of violence that would constitute a continuing threat to society. The jury found the first, but not the second, and fixed petitioner's punishment at death. . . .

We granted certiorari to consider whether a sentence of death is cruel and unusual punishment for a crime committed by a 15-year-old child. . . .

Contours of Cruel and Unusual Punishments

The authors of the Eighth Amendment [of the Constitution] drafted a categorical prohibition against the infliction of cruel and unusual punishments, but they made no attempt to define the contours of that category. They delegated that task to future generations of judges who have been guided by the "evolving standards of decency [the change over time of society's notion of acceptable behavior] that mark the progress of a maturing society." *Trop* v.

Dulles (1958). In performing that task the Court has reviewed the work product of state legislatures and sentencing juries, and has carefully considered the reasons why a civilized society may accept or reject the death penalty in certain types of cases. Thus, in confronting the question whether the youth of the defendant—more specifically, the fact that he was less than 16 years old at the time of his offense—is a sufficient reason for denying the State the power to sentence him to death, we first review relevant legislative enactments, then refer to jury determinations, and finally explain why these indicators of contemporary standards of decency confirm our judgment that such a young person is not capable of acting with the degree of culpability that can justify the ultimate penalty.

Restrictions upon Minors

Justice Powell has repeatedly reminded us of the importance of "the experience of mankind, as well as the long history of our law, recognizing that there *are* differences which must be accommodated in determining the rights and duties of children as compared with those of adults. Examples of this distinction abound in our law: in contracts, in torts, in criminal law and procedure, in criminal sanctions and rehabilitation, and in the right to vote and to hold office" *Goss* v. *Lopez* (1975) (dissenting opinion). Oklahoma recognizes this basic distinction in a number of its statutes. Thus, a minor is not eligible to vote, to sit on a jury, to marry without parental consent, or to purchase alcohol or cigarettes. Like all other States, Oklahoma has developed a juvenile justice system in which most offenders under the age of 18 are not held criminally responsible. Its statutes do provide, however, that a 16- or 17-year-old charged with murder and other serious felonies shall be considered an adult. Other than the special certification procedure that was used to authorize petitioner's trial in this case "as an adult," apparently there are no Oklahoma statutes, either civil or criminal, that treat a person under

16 years of age as anything but a "child."

The line between childhood and adulthood is drawn in different ways by various States. There is, however, complete or near unanimity among all 50 States and the District of Columbia in treating a person under 16 as a minor for several important purposes. In no State may a 15-year-old vote or serve on a jury. Further, in all but one State a 15-year-old may not drive without parental consent, and in all but four States a 15-year-old may not marry without parental consent. Additionally, in those States that have legislated on the subject, no one under age 16 may purchase pornographic materials (50 States), and in most States that have some form of legalized gambling, minors are not permitted to participate without parental consent (42 States). Most relevant, however, is the fact that all States have enacted legislation designating the maximum age for juvenile court jurisdiction at no less than 16. All of this legislation is consistent with the experience of mankind, as well as the long history of our law, that the normal 15-year-old is not prepared to assume the full responsibilities of an adult.

Minimum Age for the Death Penalty

Most state legislatures have not expressly confronted the question of establishing a minimum age for imposition of the death penalty. In 14 States, capital punishment is not authorized at all, and in 19 others capital punishment is authorized but no minimum age is expressly stated in the death penalty statute. One might argue on the basis of this body of legislation that there is no chronological age at which the imposition of the death penalty is unconstitutional and that our current standards of decency would still tolerate the execution of 10-year-old children. We think it self-evident that such an argument is unacceptable; indeed, no such argument has been advanced in this case. If, therefore, we accept the premise that some offenders are simply too young to be put to death, it is reasonable to put this group of statutes to one side because they do not focus on the question of where the chronological age line should be drawn. When we confine our attention to the 18 States that have expressly established a minimum age in their death penalty statutes, we find that all of them require that the defendant have attained at least the age of 16 at the time of the capital offense.

The conclusion that it would offend civilized standards of decency to execute a person who was less than 16 years old at the time of his or her offense is consistent with the views that have been expressed by respected professional organizations, by other nations that share our Anglo-American heritage, and by the leading members of the Western European community. Thus, the American Bar Association and the American Law Institute have formally expressed their opposition to the death penalty for juveniles. Although the death penalty has not been entirely abolished in the United Kingdom or New Zealand (it has been abolished in Australia, except in the State of New South Wales, where it is available for treason and piracy), in neither of those countries may a juvenile be executed. The death penalty has been abolished in West Germany, France, Portugal, The Netherlands, and all of the Scandinavian countries, and is available only for exceptional crimes such as treason in Canada, Italy, Spain, and Switzerland. Juvenile executions are also prohibited in the Soviet Union.

Death Sentence for Minors

The second societal factor the Court has examined in determining the acceptability of capital punishment to the American sensibility is the behavior of juries. In fact, the infrequent and haphazard handing out of death sentences by capital juries was a prime factor underlying our judgment in *Furman* v. *Georgia* (1972), that the death penalty, as then administered in unguided fashion, was unconstitutional.

While it is not known precisely how many persons have been executed during the 20th century for crimes committed under the age of 16, a scholar has recently compiled a table revealing this number to be between 18 and 20. All of these occurred during the first half of the century, with the last such execution taking place apparently in 1948. In the following year this Court observed that this "whole country has traveled far from the period in which the death sentence was an automatic and commonplace result of convictions. . . ." *Williams* v. *New York* (1949). The road we have traveled during the past four decades—in which thousands of juries have tried murder cases—leads to the unambiguous conclusion that the imposition of the death penalty on a 15-year-old offender is now generally abhorrent to the conscience of the community.

Department of Justice statistics indicate that during the years 1982 through 1986 an average of over 16,000 persons were arrested for willful criminal homicide (murder and non-negligent manslaughter) each year. Of that group of 82,094 persons, 1,393 were sentenced to death. Only 5 of them, including the petitioner in this case, were less than 16 years old at the time of the offense. Statistics of this kind can, of course, be interpreted in different ways, but they do suggest that these five young offenders have received sentences that are "cruel and unusual in the same way that being struck by lightning is cruel and unusual." *Furman* v. *Georgia* (1972).

Juvenile Culpability

"Although the judgments of legislatures, juries, and prosecutors weigh heavily in the balance, it is for us ultimately to judge whether the Eighth Amendment permits imposition of the death penalty" on one such as petitioner who committed a heinous murder when he was only 15 years old. *Enmund* v. *Florida* (1982). In making that judgment, we first ask whether the juvenile's culpability should be measured by the same standard as that of an adult, and then consider whether the application of the death penalty to this class of offenders "measurably contributes" to the social purposes that are served by the death penalty.

It is generally agreed "that punishment should be directly related to the personal culpability of the criminal defendant." *California* v. *Brown* (1987). There is also broad agreement on the proposition that adolescents as a class are less mature and responsible than adults. We stressed this difference in explaining the importance of treating the defendant's youth as a mitigating factor in capital cases:

> But youth is more than a chronological fact. It is a time and condition of life when a person may be most susceptible to influence and to psychological damage. Our history is replete with laws and judicial recognition that minors, especially in their earlier years, generally are less mature and responsible than adults. Particularly 'during the formative years of childhood and adolescence, minors often lack the experience, perspective, and judgment' expected of adults. *Bellotti* v. *Baird* (1979). *Eddings* v. *Oklahoma* (1982).

To add further emphasis to the special mitigating force of youth, Justice Powell quoted the following passage from the 1978 *Report of the Twentieth Century Fund Task Force on Sentencing Policy Toward Young Offenders*:

> Adolescents, particularly in the early and middle teen years, are more vulnerable, more impulsive, and less self-disciplined than adults. Crimes committed by youths may be just as harmful to victims as those committed by older persons, but they deserve less punishment because adolescents may have less capacity to control their conduct and to think in long-range terms than adults. Moreover, youth crime as such is not exclusively the offender's fault; offenses by the young also represent a failure of family, school, and the social system, which share responsibility for the development of America's youth.

Thus, the Court has already endorsed the proposition that less culpability should attach to a crime committed by a juvenile than to a comparable crime committed by an adult. The basis for this conclusion is too obvious to require extended explanation. Inexperience, less education, and less intelligence make the teenager less able to evaluate the consequences of his or her conduct while at the same time he or she is much more apt to be motivated by mere emotion or peer pressure than is an adult. The reasons why juveniles are not trusted with the privileges and responsibilities of an adult also explain why their irresponsible conduct is not as morally reprehensible as that of an adult.

"The death penalty is said to serve two principal social purposes: retribution and deterrence of capital crimes by prospective offenders." *Gregg* v. *Georgia* (1976). In *Gregg* we concluded that as "an expression of society's moral outrage at particularly offensive conduct," retribution was not "inconsistent with our respect for the dignity of men." Given the lesser culpability of the juvenile offender, the teenager's capacity for growth, and society's fiduciary obligations to its children, this conclusion is simply inapplicable to the execution of a 15-year-old offender.

The Deterrence Factor

For such a young offender, the deterrence rationale is equally unacceptable. The Department of Justice statistics indicate that about 98% of the arrests for willful homicide involved persons who were over 16 at the time of the offense. Thus, excluding younger persons from the class that is eligible for the death penalty will not diminish the deterrent value of capital punishment for the vast majority of potential offenders. And even with respect to those under 16 years of age, it is obvious that the potential deterrent value of the death sentence is insignificant for two reasons. The likelihood that the teenage offender has made the kind of cost-benefit analysis that attaches any weight to the possibility of execution is so remote as to be virtually nonexistent. And, even if one posits such a cold-blooded calculation by a 15-year-old, it is fanciful to believe that he would be deterred by the knowledge that a small number of persons his age have been executed during the 20th century.

In short, we are not persuaded that the imposition of the death penalty for offenses committed by persons under 16 years of age has made, or can be expected to make, any measurable contribution to the goals that capital punishment is intended to achieve. It is, therefore, "nothing more than the purposeless and needless imposition of pain and suffering," *Coker* v. *Georgia* (1977), and thus an unconstitutional punishment.

The Supreme Court's Ruling That the Death Penalty Is Cruel and Unusual Is Wrong

CAMERON TALLEY

In the following viewpoint, attorney Cameron Talley disputes the opinions of U.S. Supreme Court justices Thurgood Marshall and William J. Brennan Jr., who both have ruled that the death penalty violates the cruel and unusual punishment clause of the Eighth Amendment. Talley argues that Justice Marshall does not provide a convincing argument that the public finds the death penalty morally unacceptable or that it is an excessive punishment—two conditions that would render the penalty unconstitutional. Talley refutes Justice Brennan's argument that the framers of the Constitution were against capital punishment by noting that they specifically provided for it in the Fifth Amendment. Talley also states that Justice Brennan is mistaken in arguing that death sentences are invariably arbitrary and therefore unconstitutional because of the emotions generated in judges and juries by capital crimes. Finally, Talley argues that if society is to accord human dignity to criminals, they must receive the punishment their deeds merit rather than being treated as infants or animals incapable of

Cameron Talley, "In Favor of Capital Punishment: A Rebuttal of Abolitionist Arguments," *Western State University Law Review*, vol. 23, Spring 1996, pp. 393–439. Copyright © 1996 by the Western State University Law Review Association, Inc. Reproduced by permission.

taking responsibility for their actions. Cameron Talley is a senior deputy district attorney for Orange County, California.

Probably no two members of the Supreme Court are as revered by abolitionists [of the death penalty] as much as Justices Thurgood Marshall and William Brennan. Each used the Eighth Amendment's prohibition against "cruel and unusual punishments" to argue that the death penalty is unconstitutional. At first blush such an argument seems impossible to even attempt. After all, the Constitution's Fifth and Fourteenth Amendments specifically and approvingly refer to "capital" punishment and to a citizen being "deprived of life" as a form of punishment. Thus, it is clear that neither the Framers nor the post–Civil War Congress thought capital punishment to be unconstitutional. How then, did Marshall and Brennan argue their case?

It is instructive to examine Justice Marshall's Eighth Amendment attack against capital punishment in *Furman v. Georgia*, the 1972 landmark case in which the Supreme Court declared most of the then existing death penalty statutes unconstitutional. His argument was basically twofold. He suggested (1) that the death penalty was morally unacceptable to the public's "evolving standards of decency [the change over time of society's notion of acceptable behavior]," and (2) that it was excessive. In making these arguments Marshall first addressed the significance of the Court's prior decisions approving of the death penalty, as well as the constitutional provisions that sanctioned it:

> Perhaps the most important principle in analyzing "cruel and unusual" punishment questions is one that is reiterated again and again in the prior opinions of this Court: i.e., the cruel and unusual language "must draw its meaning from the evolving standards of decency that mark the progress of a maturing society." Thus, a penalty that was permissible at one time in our Nation's history is not necessarily permissible today.

> The fact, therefore, that the Court, or individual Justices, may have in the past expressed an opinion that the death penalty is constitutional is not now binding on us.

Marshall attempts to free himself from the constraints of constitutional text, the Framers' views on capital punishment and stare decisis. It is obvious that he is reasoning backwards in order to justify a conclusion he would reach no matter what the Constitution said. However, Marshall's reasoning to this point actually adheres to a sound tenet of constitutional adjudication: that it is necessary and proper to apply the principles found in the Constitution to the modern circumstances of a world the Framers did not and could not have known.

Standards of Decency

The impossible hurdle Marshall faces however, is to demonstrate that the application of the principle underlying the Eighth Amendment commands the result he reaches. That is, he still needs to prove that society today regards the death penalty correlatively to the way past generations regarded the rack, the thumb screw, years of hard labor spent in chains, or other "cruel and unusual" punishments. Marshall asserts this conclusion, but what actual evidence does he put forth to prove that the standards of decency have evolved such that society now considers capital punishment an unacceptable remedy for any crime? None, is the answer. All he does is survey the reasons why abolitionists such as himself disapprove of the death penalty—its potential misuse by evil prosecutors, its irrevocability, its alleged effects upon the poor and disadvantaged, etc.—and then concluded that "the average citizen," if all the facts were known to him or her concerning capital punishment, "would . . . find it shocking to his conscience and sense of justice." For Justice Marshall, this translates into a violation of the Eighth Amendment.

But during the four years that followed *Furman* citizens spoke. Their opinions were heard by their elected representatives, who in turn informed the Court that the death penalty produced no such shock to their consciences. Justice Stewart emphasized this point in his opinion for the Court in *Gregg v. Georgia*, the [1976] case in which the Supreme Court held that capital punishment is not per se unconstitutional.

The most marked indication of society's endorsement of the death penalty for murder is the legislative response to *Furman*. "The legislatures of at least 35 States have enacted new statutes authorizing the imposition of the death penalty for certain crimes, and Congress has enacted a law providing the death penalty for air piracy resulting in death." [428 U.S. 153 (1976)] The Court went on to hold that capital punishment is not per se unconstitutional.

Dissenting in *Gregg*, Justice Marshall responded to the outpouring of public opinion in support of capital punishment as follows:

> I would be less than candid if I did not acknowledge that these developments have a significant bearing on a realistic assessment of the moral acceptability of the death penalty to the American people. But if the constitutionality of the death penalty turns, as I have urged, on the opinion of an *informed* citizenry, then even the enactment of new statutes cannot be viewed as conclusive.

As evidence of the American public's ignorance about capital punishment, he goes on to cite a study which concludes that the public is uninformed about the death penalty.

Marshall's response reflects the elitist and paternalistic attitude so often exhibited by judges towards the American public. It says, in essence, "If only the unenlightened masses were as wise as I, their views would surely change."

There is a simple explanation for the flood of death penalty statutes enacted since *Furman*. The explanation is not that people are ignorant concerning capital punishment as Justice Marshall suggests. It is not that people support the death penalty "unreflectively" because it is a "symbolic or ritual institution" as professors [Franklin E.] Zimring and

[Gordon] Hawkins suggest; nor is it that Americans support capital punishment because it allows them to "demonize" murderers in whom they see their own "worst fears" and "worst desires." Ordinary citizens are touched by and concerned with heinous crimes. These ordinary citizens have concluded the appropriate punishment for those who commit such crimes is death. . . .

The Intent of the Eighth Amendment

Justice Brennan is more creative than his brother Marshall in using the Eighth Amendment as a tool against capital punishment, but ultimately he fares no better. One method he uses in attempting to circumvent the restrictions in the text of the Constitution is to simply disregard logic. In his concurring opinion in *Furman* he draws conclusions from the text and history of the Constitution that simply do not follow:

> There is, first, a textual consideration raised by the Bill of Rights itself. The Fifth Amendment declares that if a particular crime is punishable by death, a person charged with that crime is entitled to certain procedural protections. We can thus infer that the Framers recognized the existence of what was then a common punishment. We cannot, however, make the further inference that they intended to exempt this particular punishment from the express prohibition of the Cruel and Unusual Punishments Clause.

The idea is incoherent. The Framers, of course, drafted and ratified the Constitution. They could have prohibited capital punishment in that document or could have simply not mentioned it at all, leaving the subject to be addressed in another way or at another time. But the Framers did not take either of those options. Instead, they decided to specifically provide for the existence of capital punishment and to describe the procedural safeguards that should accompany it in the Fifth Amendment (and, of course, Congress did the same in the Fourteenth Amendment after the Civil

War). Hence, one cannot logically conclude, as Brennan seems to, that even though the Framers explicitly provided for capital punishment in the Fifth Amendment they simultaneously sought to prohibit it in the Eighth Amendment.

If it was to be a prohibited punishment then there would have been no need to describe how it was to be administered. But perhaps all that Brennan is trying to say here is that capital punishment is not *forever exempt* from the Cruel and Unusual Clause of the Eighth Amendment merely because it is provided for in the Fifth Amendment. Obviously this is true, but it leaves Brennan with the same problem discussed above in relation to Justice Marshall's argument: since Americans today overwhelmingly approve of capital punishment, then it cannot be placed within the purview of the Eighth Amendment because of the "evolving standards of decency." Brennan's argument goes nowhere.

Proportional Punishment

Another important Eighth Amendment objection to capital punishment is that the death penalty is "irrationally imposed" and therefore lacking in "proportionality." The Court considers two kinds of proportionality in the context of sentencing. Traditionally, the question of whether a punishment is proportional to the crime is decided by comparing the gravity of the crime committed to the severity of the punishment the offender received, as well as the punishments generally administered for other crimes, and the severity of the punishments imposed in other jurisdictions. Using this criteria the Court has held that the imposition of capital punishment is cruel and unusual for some categories of crimes. However, as Justice White explained in *Pulley v. Harris* (1984):

> [A second] sort of proportionality review presumes that the death sentence is not disproportionate to the crime in the traditional sense. It purports to inquire instead whether the penalty is nonetheless unacceptable in a particular case because [it is] disproportionate to

the punishment imposed on others convicted of the same crime.

Justice Brennan in particular has championed this argument in the capital sentencing context. In *Pulley* he states that "the irrational application of the death penalty, as evidenced by an examination of when the death penalty is actually imposed, cannot be constitutionally defended." He explains that "given the emotions generated by capital crimes, it may well be that juries, trial judges, and appellate courts considering sentences of death are invariably affected by impermissible considerations." He concludes that "although we may tolerate such irrationality in other sentencing contexts, the premise of *Furman* was that such arbitrary and capricious decision making is simply invalid when applied to 'a matter [as] grave as the determination of whether a human life should be taken or spared.'"

There are two defects in this argument. First, it simplistically misstates the law to glean from *Furman* the rule that all capital punishment schemes are required by that case to produce strict proportionality. In fact, it is difficult to distill any precise rationale from *Furman* because the five Justices who composed the majority (Douglas, Brennan, Stewart, White, and Marshall) each wrote separate opinions, as did each of the dissenters (Burger, Blackmun, Powell, and Rehnquist). Justices Brennan and Marshall reached the conclusion that the death penalty is always unconstitutional primarily on the basis of their "evolving standards of decency" argument discussed above. However, Justices Stewart, White, and Douglas "were unwilling to go so far; focusing on the procedures by which convicted defendants were selected for the death penalty rather than on the actual punishment inflicted. . . ." Obviously, the dissenters did not find either of these lines of argument compelling. Thus, of the nine Justices who sat on the Court when *Furman* was decided, only three hung their decisions on the hook of proportionality that Justice Brennan tells us was "the premise" of the case. In fairness, it must be conceded that the Court's subsequent decisions did interpret *Furman* as requiring state death penalty statutes to limit and guide a sentencer's discretion so that capital punishment would be imposed more rationally. This directive, however, concerns the sentencing *process*, and is a far cry from Brennan's assertion that *Furman* somehow requires statutes to produce strict proportionality of *results* in order to comport with the Eighth Amendment. In fact, in decisions subsequent to *Furman* the Court has insisted that states implement sentencing procedures which necessarily produce nonproportional results.

The second flaw in Brennan's argument is not constitutional, but conceptual. Even if *Furman* had stood for the proposition he claims then why on earth is Brennan willing, as he nonchalantly admits, to "tolerate such irrationality in other sentencing contexts"? It is inconsistent to assert that a process is unconstitutional for determining whether someone should be executed, but is constitutional for deciding whether someone should be locked into a cell for years, or even for life, left to suffer nightmarish degradation, pain, and decay of imprisonment.

Human Dignity

There is, finally, one last prong of the Marshall-Brennan Eighth Amendment argument which should be addressed: the stealthy "human dignity" clause. This argument contains both philosophical and constitutional components. Concerning the former, it is useful to turn first to the arguments put forth by Justice Marshall. Dissenting in *Gregg*, he writes: "The notion that retribution can serve as a moral justification for the sanction of death . . . is [a] notion that I find to be the most disturbing aspect of today's unfortunate [majority] decision." He concludes:

> To be sustained under the Eighth Amendment, the death penalty must "comport with the basic concept of human dignity at the core of the Amendment"; [and] the objective in imposing it must be "[consistent] with our respect for the dignity of other men." Under these stan-

dards, the taking of life "because the wrongdoer deserves it" surely must fall, for *such a punishment has as its very basis the total denial of the wrongdoer's dignity and worth.*

The death penalty, unnecessary to promote the goal of deterrence or to further any legitimate notion of retribution, is an excessive penalty forbidden by the Eighth and Fourteenth Amendments.

This argument is dramatically flawed because Marshall fails to consider the Kantian retributive philosophy [which holds that criminals deserve punishment and that the punishment should be equal to the harm done]. What is Marshall's answer to the proposition that a wrongdoer's human dignity and worth can *only be sustained* by imposing punishment because he "deserves it"?

Justice Brennan manages no better, explaining:

The fatal constitutional infirmity in the punishment of death is that *it treats "members of the human race as nonhumans, as objects to be toyed with and discarded.* [It is] thus inconsistent with the fundamental premise of the [Cruel and Unusual Punishment] Clause that even the vilest criminal remains a human being possessed of common human dignity."

Of course, whatever else can be said of the retributivist theory of capital punishment, the one thing it certainly does *not do* is toy with humans and treat them as nonhuman. The basic premise of the classical retributive philosophy is that humans are accorded full respect as humans by being held to account for their conduct as rational, autonomous entities. Astonishingly, Brennan fails to understand that the charge most frequently leveled *against utilitarianism* is that it is cruel and debasing because it treats men as means, not as ends (i.e., it "toys" with people and treats them as "nonhuman"). C.S. Lewis, the popular twentieth-century religious writer, articulated this Kantian idea in an article he wrote called "The Humanitarian Theory of Punishment":

To be "cured" against one's will . . . is to be put on a level with those who have not yet reached the age of reason or those who never will: to be classed with infants, imbeciles, and domestic animals. But to be punished, however severely, because we have deserved it, because we "ought to have known better," is to be treated as a human person made in God's image.

Marshall and Brennan never even address this argument in *Gregg*, nor do they address it in detail elsewhere. Perhaps Marshall touches the subject in his concurring opinion in *Furman*. He begins his attack on the retributivist philosophy dismissing it with the cursory statement: "Punishment as retribution has been condemned by scholars for centuries." He then observes:

To preserve the integrity of the Eighth Amendment, the Court has consistently denigrated retribution as a permissible goal of punishment. It is undoubtedly correct that there is a demand for vengeance on the part of many persons in a community against one who is convicted of a particularly offensive act. At times a cry is heard that morality requires vengeance to evidence society's abhorrence of the act. But the Eighth Amendment is our insulation from our baser selves. The "cruel and unusual" language limits the avenues through which vengeance can be channeled. Were this not so, the language would be empty and a return to the rack and other tortures would be possible in a given case.

Comparing Forms of Punishment

It should first be noted that the retributivist argument Marshall sets out to refute is not really a retributivist argument at all, at least not in the pure sense. It is at most a quasi-retributivist argument in that it emphasizes [Émile] Durkheim's concept of societal cohesion as the goal of punishment rather than Kant's philosophy of just deserts. In any event, Marshall's response to retributivism is again conclusory, not analytical. Explaining that the Eighth Amendment prohibits capital punishment by insulating us from our "baser selves" assumes what is to be proven. Capital punishment is in fact base, and therefore cruel and unusual. Hence, it is prohibited by the Eighth Amendment. This, however, does not explain why capital punishment is any more base or disrespectable than other forms of punishment—including locking someone into a violent, hateful, filthy prison for their entire life, a punishment that Justices Marshall and Brennan have no compunction about administering.

The last portion of Marshall's statement is not only analytically empty but misleading as well. It is empty because there is no dispute that the Eight Amendment was designed to prohibit torture and other cruel and unusual forms of punishment. Simply noting this unextraordinary fact does nothing to move forward the discussion. . . .

Another consistency in the "human dignity" argument is how could anyone object to the death penalty on grounds that it violates human dignity if they have no objection to life imprisonment? As [historian] Jacques Barzun has noted, those who favor placing murderers in prison for life do not really occupy the high moral ground in this debate, but in fact seem rather callous: "They do not see and suffer the cell, the drill, the clothes, the stench, the food; they do not feel the sexual racking of young and old bodies, the hateful promiscuity, the insane monotony, the mass degradation, the impotent hatred. . . ." Surely a life spent in prison violates human dignity as much as any method of capital punishment employed in the United States today. To remain consistent, the abolitionist cannot condone life in prison and simultaneously condemn capital punishment as violative of human dignity.

THE
HISTORY
OF
ISSUES

CHAPTER 2

The Deterrence Debate

For centuries, scholars, philosophers, jurists, and criminologists have debated whether capital punishment acts as a deterrent to crime. In describing the early deterrence debate, death penalty opponent and scholar Hugo Bedau states, "In a day when horse thievery, counterfeiting, and other crimes against property and the state were punishable by death (as they have been in more than one jurisdiction in our history), defense of the death penalty had to rest at least in part on its deterrent effect." Bedau notes that death penalty supporters today continue to argue that one of the main reasons to execute criminals is to prevent future crimes.

In the long history of the debate over capital punishment, many people have argued that in fact the threat of the punishment does not cause potential criminals to abandon their illegal intentions. In his still widely read and influential 1764 treatise *On Crimes and Punishments*, jurist Cesare Beccaria argues against the deterrent effect of the death penalty. Writing during an era when public executions were the norm, he states, "The penalty of death becomes for most men a spectacle . . . (and represents) transient pain" and is not as effective a deterrent as the "perpetual affliction" of life imprisonment. In the twentieth century criminologists John Sorensen, Robert Wrinkly, Victoria Brewer, and James Marquart studied the possible deterrent effects of the death penalty in Texas by examining crime data from 1984 to 1997. From this research, they also conclude that capital punishment is not an effective deterrent to crime.

On the other hand, those who think the death penalty deters potential criminals can also point to some illustrious thinkers who support their position. Philosopher John

Stuart Mill, in a speech delivered before the British Parliament in 1868, stated: "Who is there who knows whom it has deterred, or how many human beings it has saved who would have lived to be murderers if that awful association had not been thrown round the idea of murder from their earliest infancy?" Almost one hundred years later, former FBI director J. Edgar Hoover, who believed that "despicable crimes must be dealt with realistically," referred to capital punishment as a "time-proven deterrent" to murder.

Clearly, both those who believe and those who do not believe that the death penalty deters criminals hold strong convictions about their positions. It is therefore likely that the issue will continue to be hotly contested in the future.

The Death Penalty Is Not the Best Deterrent to Crime

CESARE BECCARIA

In his 1764 treatise On Crimes and Punishments, *Cesare Beccaria argues that the death penalty is not an effective deterrent to criminal behavior. He states that because an execution is performed quickly, it does not create a lasting impression on its viewers. The prospect of prolonged or lifelong imprisonment on the other hand, with its years of grueling labor, or even solitary confinement, is a continual—and vivid—reminder of the effects of criminal behavior. Imprisonment, argues Beccaria, is the best and truest deterrent. Beccaria, a legal scholar and proponent for legal reform, wrote his book-length essay at the age of twenty-six. Regarded as the first work to call for the abolition of the death penalty, Becarria's essay greatly influenced the European legal trends of his day and is still widely read in the twenty-first century.*

The useless profusion of punishments, which has never made men better, induces me to enquire, whether the punishment of *death* be really just or useful in a well governed state? What *right*, I ask, have men to cut the throats of their fellow-creatures? Certainly not that on which the sovereignty and laws are founded. The laws, as I have said before, are only the sum of the smallest portions of the private liberty of each individual, and represent the general

---

Cesare Beccaria, *An Essay on Crimes and Punishments*. London: F. Newberry, 1775.

will, which is the aggregate of that of each individual. Did any one ever give to others the right of taking away his life? Is it possible, that in the smallest portions of the liberty of each, sacrificed to the good of the public, can be contained the greatest of all good, life? If it were so, how shall it be reconciled to the maxim which tells us, that a man has no right to kill himself? Which he certainly must have, if he could give it away to another.

But the punishment of death is not authorized by any right; for I have demonstrated that no such right exists. It is therefore a war of a whole nation against a citizen, whose destruction they consider as necessary, or useful to the general good. But if I can further demonstrate, that it is neither necessary nor useful, I shall have gained the cause of humanity.

Only One Reason for the Death Penalty

The death of a citizen cannot be necessary, but in one case. When, though deprived of his liberty, he has such power and connections as may endanger the security of the nation; when his existence may produce a dangerous revolution in the established form of government. But even in this case, it can only be necessary when a nation is on the verge of recovering or losing its liberty; or in times of absolute anarchy, when the disorders themselves hold the place of laws. But in a reign of tranquillity; in a form of government approved by the united wishes of the nation; in a state well fortified from enemies without, and supported by strength within, and opinion, perhaps more efficacious; where all power is lodged in the hands of a true sovereign; where riches can purchase pleasures and not authority, there can be no necessity for taking away the life of a subject. . . .

Life Imprisonment Is a Better Deterrent to Crime

It is not the intenseness of the pain that has the greatest effect on the mind but its continuance; for our sensibility is more easily and more powerfully affected by weak but repeated impressions, than by a violent, but momentary, impulse. The power of habits is universal over every sensible being. As it is by that we learn to speak, to walk, and to satisfy our necessities, so the ideas of morality are stamped on our minds by repeated impressions. The death of a criminal is a terrible but momentary spectacle, and therefore a less efficacious method of deterring others, than the continued example of a man deprived of his liberty, condemned, as a beast of burthen, to repair, by his labour, the injury he has done to society. *If I commit such a crime*, says the spectator to himself, *I shall be reduced to that miserable condition for the rest of my life.* A much more powerful preventive than the fear of death, which men always behold in distant obscurity.

The terrors of death make so slight an impression, that it has not force enough to withstand the forgetfulness natural to mankind, even in the most essential things; especially when assisted by the passions. . . .

The execution of a criminal is, to the multitude, a spectacle, which in some excites compassion mixed with indignation. These sentiments occupy the mind much more than that salutary terror which the laws endeavour to inspire; but in the contemplation of continued suffering, terror is the only, or a least predominant sensation. The severity of a punishment should be just sufficient to excite compassion in the spectators, as it is intended more for them than for the criminal.

A punishment, to be just, should have only that degree of severity which is sufficient to deter others. Now there is no man, who upon the least reflection, would put in competition total and perpetual loss of his liberty, with the greatest advantages he could possibly obtain in consequence of a crime. Perpetual slavery [life imprisonment] then, has in it all that is necessary to deter the most hardened and determined, as much as the punishment of death. I say it has more. There are many who can look upon death with intrepidity and firmness; some through fanaticism, and others through vanity, which attends us even to the grave; others from a desperate resolution, either to get rid of their misery, or cease to live: but fanaticism and vanity forsake the criminal in slavery, in chains and fetters, in an iron cage; and despair seems rather the beginning than the end of their misery. The mind, by collecting itself and uniting all its force, can, for a moment, repel assailing grief; but its most vigorous efforts are insufficient to resist perpetual wretchedness.

In all nations, where death is used as a punishment, every example supposes a new crime committed. Whereas in perpetual slavery, every criminal affords a frequent and lasting example; and if it be necessary that men should often be witnesses of the power of the laws, criminals should often be put to death; but this supposes a frequency of crimes; and from hence this punishment will cease to have its effect, so that it must be useful and useless at the same time.

I shall be told, that perpetual slavery is as painful a punishment as death, and therefore as cruel. I answer, that if all the miserable moments in the life of a slave were collected into one point, it would be a more cruel punishment than any other; but these are scattered through his whole life, whilst the pain of death exerts all its force in a moment. There is also another advantage in the punishment of slavery, which is, that it is more terrible to the spectator than to the sufferer himself; for the spectator considers the sum of all his wretched moments, whilst the sufferer, by the misery of the present, is prevented from thinking of the future. All evils are increased by the imagination, and the sufferer finds resources and consolations, of which the spectators are ignorant; who judge by their own sensibility of what passes in a mind, by habit grown callous to misfortune.

Let us, for a moment, attend to the reasoning of a robber or assassin, who is deterred from violating the laws by the gibbet or the wheel. I am sensible, that to develop the sentiments of one's own heart, is an art which education only can teach: but although a villain may not be able to give a clear account of his principles, they nevertheless influence his conduct. He reasons thus:

> What are these laws, that I am bound to respect, which make so great a difference between me and the rich man? He refuses me the farthing I ask of him, and excuses himself, by bidding me have recourse to labour with which he is unacquainted. Who made these laws? The rich and the great, who never deigned to visit the miserable hut of the poor; who have never seen him dividing a piece of mouldly bread, amidst the cries of his famished children and the tears of his wife. Let us break those ties, fatal to the greatest part of mankind, and only useful to a few indolent tyrants. Let us attack injustice at its source. I will return to my natural state of independence. I shall live free and happy on the fruits of my courage and industry. A day of pain and repentance may come, but it will be short; and for an hour of grief I shall enjoy years of pleasure and liberty. King of a small number, as determined as myself, I will correct the mistakes of fortune; and I shall see those tyrants grow pale and tremble at the sight of him, whom, with insulting pride, they would not suffer to rank with their dogs and horses.

Religion then presents itself to the mind of this lawless villain, and promising him almost a certainty of eternal happiness upon the easy terms of repentance, contributes much to lessen the horror of the last scene of the tragedy.

But he who foresees, that he must pass a great number of years, even his whole life, in pain and slavery; a slave to those laws by which he was protected; in sight of his fellow citizens, with whom he lives in freedom and society; makes an useful comparison between those evils, the uncertainty of his success, and the shortness of the time in which he shall enjoy the fruits of his transgression. The example of those wretches continually before his eyes, make a much greater impression on him than a punishment, which, instead of correcting, makes him more obdurate.

The punishment of death is pernicious to society, from the example of barbarity it affords. If the passions, or the necessity of war, have taught men to shed the blood of their fellow creatures, the laws, which are intended to moderate the ferocity of mankind, should not increase it by examples of barbarity, the more horrible, as this punishment is usually attended with formal pageantry. Is it not absurd, that the laws, which detest and punish homicide, should, in order to prevent murder, publicly commit murder themselves?

The Death Penalty Deters Potential Murderers

JOHN STUART MILL

In 1868 the British Parliament was engaged in a debate over a proposed bill banning capital punishment. The death penalty had been abolished for all crimes except aggravated murder (murder combined with specific acts, or against certain public officials, or against a certain class of victim). Philosopher John Stuart Mill (1806–1873) delivered a speech before Parliament on April 21, 1868, in opposition to the bill, asking the legislators to retain the death penalty for what he described as "the greatest crime known to the law." Mill begins his argument by describing the death penalty as the least cruel method by which to deter the crime of murder. He offers a detailed discourse on the humanity of a swift execution (as opposed to the misery of an extended or life imprisonment). Mill concludes by explaining that the willingness of the state to take a human life in punishment shows how much the state values the lives of its citizens in general. Mill was a prominent philosopher, political economist, and leading proponent of utilitarianism, which advocates those actions that grant the greatest amount of happiness to the largest number of people. His major writings include A System of Logic *(1843),* Principles of Political Economy *(1848),* On Liberty *(1859),* Considerations on Representative Government *(1861),* Utilitarianism *(1863), and* The Subjection of Women *(1869).*

John Stuart Mill, *Hansard's Parliamentary Debate*, 3rd series, London, April 21, 1868.

It is always a matter of regret to me to find myself, on a public question, opposed to those who are called—sometimes in the way of honour, and sometimes in what is intended for ridicule—the philanthropists. Of all persons who take part in public affairs, they are those for whom, on the whole, I feel the greatest amount of respect; for their characteristic is, that they devote their time, their labour, and much of their money to objects purely public, with a less admixture of either personal or class selfishness, than any other class of politicians whatever. On almost all the great questions, scarcely any politicians are so steadily and almost uniformly to be found on the side of right; and they seldom err, but by an exaggerated application of some just and highly important principle. On the very subject that is now occupying us we all know what signal service they have rendered. It is through their efforts that our criminal laws . . . have so greatly relaxed their most revolting and most impolitic ferocity, that aggravated murder is now practically the only crime which is punished with death by any of our lawful tribunals; and we are even now deliberating whether the extreme penalty should be retained in that solitary case. This vast gain, not only to humanity, but to the ends of penal justice, we owe to the philanthropists; and if they are mistaken, as I cannot but think they are, in the present instance, it is only in not perceiving the right time and place for stopping in a career hitherto so eminently beneficial. Sir, there is a point at which, I conceive, that career ought to stop.

In Defense of the Death Penalty

When there has been brought home to any one, by conclusive evidence, the greatest crime known to the law; and when the attendant circumstances suggest no palliation of the guilt, no hope that the culprit may even yet not be unworthy to live among mankind, nothing to make it probable that the crime was an exception to his general character rather than a consequence of it, then I confess it appears to me that to deprive the criminal of the life of which he has proved himself to be unworthy—solemnly to blot him out from the fellowship of mankind and from the catalogue of the living—is the most appropriate, as it is certainly the most impressive, mode in which society can attach to so great a crime the penal consequences which for the security of life it is indispensable to annex to it. I defend this penalty, when confined to atrocious cases, on the very ground on which it is commonly attacked—on that of humanity to the criminal; as beyond comparison the least cruel mode in which it is possible adequately to deter from the crime. If, in our horror of inflicting death, we endeavour to devise some punishment for the living criminal which shall act on the human mind with a deterrent force at all comparable to that of death, we are driven to inflictions less severe indeed in appearance, and therefore less efficacious, but far more cruel in reality.

Few, I think, would venture to propose, as a punishment for aggravated murder, less than imprisonment with hard labour for life; that is the fate to which a murderer would be consigned by the mercy which shrinks from putting him to death. But has it been sufficiently considered what sort of a mercy this is, and what kind of life it leaves to him? If, indeed, the punishment is not really inflicted—if it becomes the sham which a few years ago such punishments were rapidly becoming—then, indeed, its adoption would be almost tantamount to giving up the attempt to repress murder altogether. But if it really is what it professes to be, and if it is realized in all its rigour by the popular imagination, as it very probably would not be, but as it must be if it is to be efficacious, it will be so shocking that when the memory of the crime is no longer fresh, there will be almost insuperable difficulty in executing it. What comparison can there really be, in point of severity, between consigning a man to the short pang of a rapid death, and immuring him in a living tomb, there to linger out what may be a long life in the hardest and most monotonous toil, without any of its alleviations or rewards—debarred from all pleasant sights and sounds, and cut off from all earthly hope, except a slight mitigation of bodily restraint, or a small improvement of diet? Yet even such a lot as this, because there is no one moment at which the suffering is of terrifying intensity, and, above all, because it does not contain the element, so imposing to the imagination, of the unknown, is universally reputed a milder punishment than death—stands in all codes as a mitigation of the capital penalty, and is thankfully accepted as such. For it is characteristic of all punishments which depend on duration for their efficacy—all, therefore, which are not corporal or pecuniary—that they are more rigorous than they seem; while it is, on the contrary, one of the strongest recommendations a punishment can have, that it should seem more rigorous than it is; for its practical power depends far less on what it is than on what it seems.

There is not, I should think, any human infliction which makes an impression on the imagination so entirely out of proportion to its real severity as the punishment of death. The punishment must be mild indeed which does not add more to the sum of human misery than is necessarily or directly added by the execution of a criminal. . . . The most that human laws can do to anyone in the matter of death is to hasten it; the man would have died at any rate; not so very much later, and on the average, I fear, with a considerably greater amount of bodily suffering. Society is asked, then, to denude itself of an instrument of punishment which, in the grave cases to which alone it is suitable, effects its purpose at a less cost of human suffering than any other; which, while it inspires more terror, is less cruel in actual fact than any punishment that we should think of substituting for it. My hon. Friend [Mr. Gilpin] says that it does not inspire terror, and that experience proves it to be a failure. But the influence of a punishment is not to be estimated by its effect on hardened criminals. Those whose habitual way of life keeps them, so to speak, at all times within sight of the gallows, do grow to care less about it; as, to compare good things with bad, an old soldier is not much affected by the chance of dying in battle. I can afford to admit all that is often said about the indifference of professional criminals to the gallows. Though of that indifference one-third is probably bravado and another third confidence that they shall have the luck to escape, it is quite probable that the remaining third is real. But the efficacy of a punishment which acts principally through the imagination, is chiefly to be measured by the impression it makes on those who are still innocent: by the horror with which it surrounds the first promptings of guilt; the restraining influence it exercises over the beginning of the thought which, if indulged, would become a temptation; the check which it exerts over the gradual declension towards the state—never suddenly attained—in which crime no longer revolts, and punishment no longer terrifies.

The Effects of Punishment

As for what is called the failure of death punishment, who is able to judge of that? We partly know who those are whom it has not deterred; but who is there who knows whom it has deterred, or how many human beings it has saved who would have lived to be murderers if that awful association had not been thrown round the idea of murder from their earliest infancy? Let us not forget that the most imposing fact loses its power over the imagination if it is made too cheap. When a punishment fit only for the most atrocious crimes is lavished on small offences until human feeling recoils from it, then, indeed, it ceases to intimidate, because it ceases to be believed in.

The failure of capital punishment in cases of theft is easily accounted for: the thief did not believe that it would be inflicted. He had learnt by experience that jurors would perjure themselves rather than find him guilty; that Judges would seize any excuse for not sentencing him to death, or for recommending him to mercy; and that if neither jurors nor Judges were merciful, there were still hopes from an authority above both. When things had come to this pass it was high time to give up the vain attempt. When it is impossible to inflict a punishment, or when its infliction becomes a public scandal, the idle threat cannot too soon disappear from the statute book. And in the case of the host of offences which were formerly capital, I heartily rejoice that it did become impracticable to execute the law.

If the same state of public feeling comes to exist in the case of murder; if the time comes when jurors refuse to find a murderer guilty; when Judges will not sentence him to death, or will recommend him to mercy; or when, if juries and Judges do not flinch from their duty, Home Secretaries, under pressure of deputations and memorials, shrink from theirs, and the threat becomes, as it became in the other cases, a mere *brutum fulmen;* then, indeed, it may become necessary to do in this case what has been done in those—to abrogate the penalty. That time may come—my hon. Friend thinks that it has nearly come. I hardly know whether he lamented it or boasted of it; but he and his Friends are entitled to the boast: for if it comes it will be their doing, and they will have gained what I cannot but call a fatal victory, for they will have achieved it by bringing about, if they will forgive me for saying so, an enervation, an effeminacy, in the general mind of the country. For what else than effeminacy is it to be so much more shocked by taking a man's life than by depriving him of all that makes life desirable or valuable? Is death, then, the greatest of all earthly ills? *Usque adeone mori miserum est?* [Is it, indeed, so dreadful a thing to die?] Has it not been from of old one chief part of a manly education to make us despise death—teaching us to account it, if an evil at all, by no means high in the list of evils; at all events, as an inevitable one, and to hold, as it were, our lives in our hands, ready to be given or risked at any moment, for a sufficiently worthy object? I am sure that my hon. Friends know all this as well, and have as much of all these feelings as any of the rest of us; possibly more. But I cannot think that this is likely to be the effect of their teaching on the general mind. . . .

The Value of Human Life

Much has been said of the sanctity of human life, and the absurdity of supposing that we can teach respect for life by ourselves destroying it. But I am surprised at the employment of this argument, for it is one which might be brought against any punishment whatever. It is not human life only, not human life as such, that ought to be sacred to us, but human feelings. The human capacity of suffering is what we should cause to be respected, not the mere capacity of existing. And we may imagine somebody asking how we can teach people not to inflict suffering by ourselves inflicting it? But to this I should answer—all of us would answer—that to deter by suffering from inflicting suffering is not only possible, but the very purpose of penal justice. Does fining a criminal show want of respect for property, or imprisoning him, for personal freedom? Just as unreasonable is it to think that to take the life of a man who has taken that of another is to show want of regard for human life. We show, on the contrary, most emphatically our regard for it, by the adoption of a rule that he who violates that right in another forfeits it for himself, and that while no other crime that he can commit deprives him of his right to live, this shall.

There is one argument against capital punishment, even in extreme cases, which I cannot deny to have weight. . . . It is this—that if by an error of justice an innocent person is put to death, the mistake can never be corrected; all compensation, all reparation for the wrong is impossible. This would be indeed a serious objection if these miserable mistakes—among the most tragical occurrences in the whole round of human affairs—could not be made extremely rare. The argument is invincible where the mode of criminal procedure is dangerous to the innocent, or where the Courts of Justice are not trusted. And this probably is the reason why the objection to an irreparable punishment began (as I believe it did) earlier, and is more intense and more widely diffused, in some parts of the Continent of Europe than it is here. There are on the continent great and enlightened countries, in which the criminal procedure is not so favourable to innocence, does not afford the same security against erroneous conviction, as it does among us; countries where the Courts of Justice seem to think they fail in their duty unless they find somebody guilty; and in their really laudable desire to hunt guilt from its hiding-places, expose themselves to a serious danger of condemning the innocent. If our own procedure and Courts of Justice afforded ground for similar apprehension, I should be the first to join in withdrawing the power of inflicting irreparable punishment from such tribunals. But we all know that the defects of our procedure are the very opposite.

Our rules of evidence are even too favourable to the prisoner: and juries and Judges carry out the maxim, "It is better that ten guilty should escape than that one innocent person should suffer," not only to the letter, but beyond the letter. Judges are most anxious to point out and juries to allow for, the barest possibility of the prisoner's innocence. No human judgment is infallible: such sad cases as my hon. Friend cited will sometimes occur; but in so grave a case as that of murder, the accused, in our system, has always the benefit of the merest shadow of a doubt. And this suggests another consideration very germane to the question. The very fact that death punishment is more shocking than any other to the imagination, necessarily renders the courts of Justice more scrupulous in requiring the fullest evidence of guilt. Even that which is the greatest objection to capital punishment, the impossibility of correcting an error once committed, must make, and does make, juries and Judges more careful in forming their opinion, and more jealous in their scrutiny of the evidence.

If the substitution of penal servitude for death in cases of murder should cause any relaxation in this conscientious scrupulosity, there would be a great evil to set against the real, but I hope rare, advantage of being able to make reparation to a condemned person who was afterwards discovered to be innocent. In order that the possibility of correction may be kept open wherever the chance of his sad contingency is more than infinitesimal, it is quite right that the Judge should recommend to the Crown a commutation of the sentence, not solely when the proof of guilt is open to the smallest suspicion, but whenever there remains anything unexplained and mysterious in the case, raising a desire for more light, or making it likely that further information may at some future time be obtained.

Against Total Abolition

I would also suggest that whenever the sentence is commuted the grounds of the commutation should, in some authentic form, be made known to the public. Thus much I willingly concede to my hon. Friend; but on the question of total abolition I am inclined to hope that the feeling of the country is not with him, and that the limitation of death punishment to the cases referred to in the Bill of last year [1867] will be generally considered sufficient. The mania which existed a short time ago for paring down all our punishments seems to have reached its limits, and not before it was time. We were in danger of being left without any effectual punishment, except for small offences. . . .

I think . . . that in the case of most offences, except those against property, there is more need of strengthening our punishments than of weakening them: and that severer sentences, with an apportionment of them to the different kinds of offences which shall approve itself better than at present to the moral sentiments of the community, are the kind of reform of which our penal system now stands in need.

The Death Penalty Deters Juries from Convicting Murderers

MAYNARD SHIPLEY

Discussions of deterrence usually focus on whether the death penalty deters criminal behavior. However, in the following selection, Maynard Shipley discusses whether the death penalty deters juries from convicting people of crimes. Using data from various states that have abolished the death penalty, he compares the conviction rates of murder defendants before and after the states abolished capital punishment. Shipley concludes that defendants in murder cases are more likely to be convicted when the penalty is life imprisonment rather than the death penalty. Maynard Shipley wrote this article for the American Law Review *in 1909. He served as editor of the* Commonwealth, *a socialist weekly newspaper, from 1913 to 1914. In 1920, Shipley was the Socialist Party candidate for U.S. Representative in California's Sixth District.*

I t used to be asked in all seriousness, "Does capital punishment prevent murders?" As the death penalty is no longer systematically applied, the discussion must now be confined to the more pertinent question, "Does the insti-

Maynard Shipley, "Does Capital Punishment Prevent Convictions?" *American Law Review*, vol. 43, May/June 1909.

tution of capital punishment prevent convictions?" Or, to put the same problem in another form, "Does the menace of the death penalty tend more to protect the accused prisoner through intimidation of the jury, than to protect society through its supposed deterrent effect upon the would-be assassin?"

Henry Ward Beecher long ago observed that "while the fear of hanging does not deter men from crime, the fear of inflicting death deters many a jury from finding a just verdict, and favors the escape of criminals."

Not only is the evidence in favor of a prisoner doubly reckoned in trials involving capital punishment, but, as the editor of a prominent periodical recently declared: "The present system, by which criminals are allowed incalculable delays, obstructive methods, and benefits of reasonable doubts, is kept in vogue by the existence of the death sentence more than by any other single fact."

To the disadvantages already mentioned must be added the enormous fees and other expenditures incident to murder trials, which would, in many cases, be materially reduced were imprisonment, rather than death, the threatened penalty. With these facts in view, the recent revival of legislative activity on the question of abolishing the death penalty becomes of vital importance, not only to jurists and legislators, but to the public at large. It may not, therefore, be without interest to review briefly some data which tend to show what effect abolition of the gallows in certain states of our Union has had upon the administration of justice in these communities.

Obtaining Convictions in Michigan

As Michigan was the first state in the Union to permanently abolish the death penalty (1848), the experiment was watched with a great deal of interest, both in this country and abroad. Fortunately for our present purposes, a letter of inquiry was addressed to Governor Austin Blair, by a member of the British Parliament, asking for information as to the results of the substitution of life imprisonment for capital punishment in that state. In his reply, among other expressions of satisfaction, Governor Blair said, "Before the abolition of the death penalty murders were not unfrequent, but convictions were rarely or never obtained. . . . Convictions and punishment are now much more certain than before the change was made. . . . The reform has been successfully tried, and is no longer an experiment."

The late Professor T.M. Cooley, who was for many years Dean of the Law School of the University of Michigan, and who served thirteen years on the Supreme Bench of that State, said of capital punishment: "This State has dispensed with it for a third of a century, and I can only say of the result that, in my opinion, human life within its jurisdiction has been at least as secure against criminal assaults as in any of the adjacent states where the death penalty has been retained. The fear of the penalty, in my opinion, deters persons from taking life in very rare and peculiar cases only, if in any, and the greater certainty of conviction and punishment when imprisonment is substituted fully counterbalances any benefit that can come from fear."

That convictions for murder in the first degree are more difficult to obtain in those states which retain the death penalty for this crime is evidenced by the fact that while 28.2 per cent. of the 138 persons indicted on this charge in Michigan were convicted, during a period of three years, in Massachusetts during the same time, but 10 per cent. of such indictments resulted in convictions of murder in the first degree, and in Ohio the percentage was still lower.

Obtaining Convictions in Rhode Island

Encouraged by the increase of convictions and decrease of murders following abolishment of the death penalty in Michigan, and agitated by the discovery that an innocent man had just been executed at the hands of the public hangman, the legislators of Rhode Island, in 1852, enacted a law which limited capital punishment to condemned murderers who should attack their keepers. The facts go to show that in Rhode Island, as in Michigan, the ends of justice were better served after abolishment of capital punishment. We have the direct testimony of Governor Wye on this point. Writing in 1864, he said: "Although opposed to the present law when passed, I am equally opposed to a change in it until the experiment has been tried long enough to satisfy us that it has failed. I am clearly of opinion that the present state of the law is sustained by public opinion. . . . My observation fully justifies me in saying that conviction for murder is far more certain now in proper cases than when death was the punishment for it."

The late Professor Francis Wayland, Dean of the Yale Law School, found that in the most populous county of Rhode Island, Providence, the proportion of convictions to trials for murder in the first degree exceeded 50 per cent. during the thirty years succeeding abrogation of the death penalty; and Mr. Andrew Palm, in his well-known work on "The Penalty of Death," states that the convictions for murder in Rhode Island were 65 per cent. of the number tried, as compared with 17 per cent. in Massachusetts during the same period.

Obtaining Convictions in Wisconsin

That the abolition of capital punishment in Wisconsin, as early as 1853, was largely due to the extreme difficulty experienced in securing convictions in murder trials is attested by a letter addressed to Mr. John Bright, M.P., from the pen of Governor J.E. Lewes, written in 1864, in which he states that: "the great aversion of many to the taking of life, rendering it almost impossible to obtain jurors from the more intelligent portion of the community, the liability of the innocent to suffer so extreme a penalty and be beyond the reach of the pardoning power, and the disposition of courts and juries not to convict, . . . convinced me that this relic of barbarism should be abolished."

Of nine states from which the statistics of indictments

and convictions for murder in the first degree could be obtained for a period of three years, Wisconsin showed the highest proportion of convictions to prosecutions, namely, 40.5 per cent. During the same period, in Idaho, of 21 persons indicted for murder in the first degree, not a single one was convicted as charged.

As early as 1869, Hon. Thomas B. Reed delivered a speech before the Maine legislature asking for abolition of the death penalty, on the ground that though capital punishment was not an effective measure for prevention of crime, it was all too efficient as a preventive of convictions. It was not, however, until after the erroneous conviction of Stain and Cromwell, who had been sentenced for murder which someone else had perpetrated, that public opinion in Maine became thoroughly enough aroused on the question to cause abolition of the death penalty, in 1876. Official statistics, compiled by the Attorney-General show that of 227 persons on trial for homicide during the seventeen years, 1860–76, 35 only, or 15.4 per cent., were convicted; while during a period of twenty years subsequently to the abolishment of capital punishment, the proportion of convictions to prosecutions rose to 64.5 per cent. This record may be better appreciated when it is stated that in the United States Courts the ratio of convictions to trials for homicide averaged but 16.6 per cent. during the three years ending with 1892. In the State and Federal courts of the entire United States convictions follow homicides in about 25 per cent. of the cases reported.

Obtaining Convictions in Colorado

During four years the death penalty was legally abolished in Colorado, and then partially restored in 1901 by a law giving the jury the right to decide in its verdict whether the penalty shall be life imprisonment or death by hanging. In his report to the United States Prison Commissioner, Mr. C.L. Stonaker, Secretary of the State Board of Charities and Correction, said, in 1900: "Capital punishment has been abolished in this state without any apparent increase in the number of murders committed, but with a better showing for speedy trials and convictions. Since the establishment of the law abolishing capital punishment, 50 per cent. of murder trials have resulted in convictions."...

From the facts already presented with reference to the administration of justice before and after abolishment of capital punishment in Michigan, Wisconsin, Rhode Island, Maine, and Colorado, it seems evident that convictions followed murders with greater certainty after life imprisonment was made the supreme penalty.

The Death Penalty Is Necessary to Protect Society

J. EDGAR HOOVER

As the director of one of the premier law enforcement agencies in the United States—the Federal Bureau of Investigation—J. Edgar Hoover was an ardent supporter of capital punishment. In the following selection, Hoover defends the death penalty as part of the "realistic punishment" the public expects from its law enforcers. He also refutes the argument that it is better to rehabilitate murderers than to execute them. He argues instead that capital punishment is one of the "time-proven deterrents" to murder and other capital crimes. J. Edgar Hoover served as director of the FBI from 1924 until his death in 1972 at the age of seventy-seven. During his tenure, the FBI developed a world-renowned fingerprint file and crime-detection laboratory.

Part I

The question of capital punishment has sent a storm of controversy thundering across our Nation—millions of spoken and written words seek to examine the question so that decisions may be reached which befit our civilization.

The struggle for answers concerning the taking of men's lives is one to which every American should lend his voice, for the problem in a democracy such as ours is not

Part I: J. Edgar Hoover, *FBI Law Enforcement Bulletin*, vol. 29, June 1960. Part II: J. Edgar Hoover, *FBI Law Enforcement Bulletin*, vol. 30, June 1961. Part III: J. Edgar Hoover, *Uniform Crime Reports*, 1959.

one for a handful of men to solve alone.

As a representative of law enforcement, it is my belief that a great many of the most vociferous cries for abolition of capital punishment emanate from those areas of our society which have been insulated against the horrors man can and does perpetrate against his fellow beings. Certainly, penetrative and searching thought must be given before considering any blanket cessation of capital punishment in a time when unspeakable crimes are being committed. The savagely mutilated bodies and mentally ravaged victims of murderers, rapists and other criminal beasts beg consideration when the evidence is weighed on both sides of the scales of Justice.

At the same time, nothing is so precious in our country as the life of a human being, whether he is a criminal or not, and on the other side of the scales must be placed all of the legal safeguards which our society demands.

Experience has clearly demonstrated, however, that the time-proven deterrents to crime are sure detection, swift apprehension, and proper punishment. Each is a necessary ingredient. Law-abiding citizens have a right to expect that the efforts of law enforcement officers in detecting and apprehending criminals will be followed by realistic punishment.

Serving the Public Interest

It is my opinion that when no shadow of a doubt remains relative to the guilt of a defendant, the public interest demands capital punishment be invoked where the law so provides.

Who, in all good conscience, can say that Julius and Ethel Rosenberg, the spies who delivered the secret of the atomic bomb into the hands of the Soviets, should have been spared when their treachery caused the shadow of annihilation to fall upon all of the world's peoples? What place would there have been in civilization for these two who went to their deaths unrepentant, unwilling to the last to help their own country and their own fellow men? What would have been the chances of rehabilitating Jack Gilbert

Graham, who placed a bomb in his own mother's luggage and blasted her and forty-three other innocent victims into oblivion as they rode an airliner across a peaceful sky?

A judge once said, "The death penalty is a warning, just like a lighthouse throwing its beams out to sea. We hear about shipwrecks, but we do not hear about the ships the lighthouse guides safely on their way. We do not have proof of the number of ships it saves, but we do not tear the lighthouse down."

Despicable crimes must be dealt with realistically. To abolish the death penalty would absolve other Rosenbergs and Grahams from fear of the consequences for committing atrocious crimes. Where the death penalty is provided, a criminal's punishment may be meted out commensurate with his deeds. While a Power transcending man is the final Judge, this same Power gave man reason so that he might protect himself. Capital punishment is an instrument with which he may guard the righteous against the predators among men.

We must never allow misguided compassion to erase our concern for the hundreds of unfortunate, innocent victims of bestial criminals.

Part II

Refuting Arguments Against the Death Penalty

The capital punishment question, in which law enforcement officers have a basic interest, has been confused recently by self-styled agitators "against the evil of capital punishment." A brochure released not long ago, pleading for "rehabilitation" of murderers while passing lightly over the plight of the killers' innocent victims and families, charges that law enforcement officers "become so insensitized by their dealings with vicious criminals that they go to the extreme of feeling that the death penalty is absolutely necessary."

To add to the burden of conscience borne by peace officers, prosecutors, and jurists and to brand law enforcement officers as callous, unfeeling men "insensitized" to the sanctity of human life are gross acts of injustice to these servants of the public. This ridiculous allegation is mutely refuted by the compassion which wells up in quiet tears flowing down the cheeks of hardened, veteran officers who too often see the ravaged bodies of victims of child molesters.

There can be no doubt of the sincerity of many of those who deplore capital punishment. A realistic approach to the problem, however, demands that they weigh the right of innocent persons to live their lives free from fear of bestial killers against statistical arguments which boast of how few murderers kill again after "rehabilitation" and release. No one, unless he can probe the mind of every potential killer, can say with any authority whatsoever that capital punishment is not a deterrent. As one police officer has asked, how can these "authorities" possibly know how many people are not on death row because of the deterrent effect of executions? . . .

Moral Necessity of Capital Punishment

The proponents of "rehabilitation" for all murderers quote those portions of the Bible which they believe support their lavender-and-old-lace world where evil is neither recognized nor allowed. But the Bible clearly reveals that enforcement of moral justice is nothing new to our age. In fact, in referring to man as the "image of God," the Old Testament, so freely quoted by opponents of the death penalty, also states, "Whoso sheddeth man's blood, by man shall his blood be shed: for in the image of God made he man." (Genesis 9:6) There are many passages in the Old Testament which refer to capital punishment being necessary to enforce the laws of society. Since the Old Testament was written about and to a nation while the New Testament was written to individuals and to a nonpolitical body known as the Church, there is a difference in emphasis and approach. Certainly, however, the moral laws of the Old Testament remain with us today.

Misguided do-gooders frequently quote the Sixth Commandment, "Thou shalt not kill," to prove that capital punishment is wrong. This Commandment in the twentieth chapter, verse 13, of Exodus has also been interpreted to mean: "Thou shalt do no murder." Then the twenty-first chapter, verse 12, says, "He that smiteth a man, so that he die, shall be surely put to death." We can no more change the application to our society of this basic moral law in the Old Testament than we can change the meaning of Leviticus 19:18: "thou shalt love thy neighbor as thyself," which Jesus quoted in the New Testament.

To "love thy neighbor" is to protect him; capital punishment acts as at least one wall to afford "God's children" protection.

Part III

Deterrent Effects of Capital Punishment

Most states have capital punishment; a few do not. For the most part, capital punishment is associated with the crime of murder. Some states have high murder rates; some do not. Of those states with low murder rates, some have capital punishment; some do not. The number of murders that occur within a state as indicated by rates is due to a wide range of social, human and material factors.

It would be convenient for a study of the effects of capital punishment as a deterrent if states fell neatly into two groups: (1) those with low murder rates and capital punishment; and (2) those with high murder rates and no capital punishment. Or, if the user of these statistics is making a case against capital punishment, he would prefer to demonstrate that the states with low murder rates are those that do not have capital punishment. But to expect such an oversimplification of a highly complex subject is to engage in wishful thinking or a futile groping for proof that is not there.

Some who propose the abolishment of capital punishment select statistics that "prove" their point and ignore those that point the other way. Comparisons of murder rates between the nine states which abolished the death penalty or qualified its use and the forty-one states which have retained it either individually, before or after abolition, or by group are completely inconclusive.

The professional law enforcement officer is convinced from experience that the hardened criminal has been and is deterred from killing based on the prospect of the death penalty. It is possible that the deterrent effect of capital punishment is greater in states with a high murder rate if the conditions which contribute to the act of murder develop more frequently in those states. For the law enforcement officer the time-proven deterrents to crime are sure detection, swift apprehension, and proper punishment. Each is a necessary ingredient.

Statistics Can Neither Prove nor Disprove That Capital Punishment Deters Murderers

JAMES Q. WILSON

In this excerpt from his book Thinking About Crime, *James Q. Wilson examines the difficulty in assessing the deterrent effects (or lack thereof) of capital punishment. Analyzing various types of statistical studies, Wilson finds weaknesses inherent in all of them, including a lack of consistency in the way each study defines the death penalty and the widely different types of capital crimes that are examined in each study. He concludes that sufficient evidence will probably never be available to prove whether capital punishment deters murderers. Wilson is considered one of the leading authors on crime in America. He has written numerous books, including* The Investigators: Managing the FBI and Narcotics Agents *(1978) and* Crime and Human Nature *(1998). He also edited* Crime: Public Policies for Crime Control *(2002). Wilson has been a professor at Harvard University since 1977.*

Perhaps the first serious effort in this country to assess the deterrent effect of the death penalty was that of

Thorsten Sellin, an opponent of capital punishment. In his first study [in 1967], he did four things. First, he compared homicide rates between adjacent states with and without the death penalty. The crude rates for homicide in these groups of states appeared to be about the same and to change in the same ways, regardless of whether a state did or did not have the death penalty on the books. Second, he compared homicide rates within states before and after they abolished or restored the death penalty. The rates did not change significantly after the legal status of the penalties changed. Third, he examined homicide rates in those cities where executions occurred and were presumed to have been publicized. There was no difference in the homicide rates in those cities where executions occurred and were presumed to have been publicized. There was no difference in the homicide rate before and after the executions. (Similar studies, with similar results, were done by Robert Dann, Leonard D. Savitz, and William Graves. Graves even uncovered evidence in California that led him to speculate that there was an increase in the number of homicides on the days immediately preceding an execution.) Finally, Sellin sought to discover whether law-enforcement officers were safer from murderous attacks in states with the death penalty than in those without it. He found that the rate at which police officers were shot and killed in states that had abolished capital punishment was the same as the rate in states that had retained the death penalty. Donald R. Campion reached the same conclusion after studying the deaths of state police officers.

It is sometimes argued in rejoinder to these findings that while executions may not deter murderers generally, they will help protect prison guards and other inmates from fatal assaults by convicts who "have nothing else to lose." Sellin compiled a list of fifty-nine persons who committed murders in state and federal prisons in 1965. He concluded that it is "visionary" to believe that the death penalty could reduce the "hazards of life in prison." Eleven of the prison murders were found in states without capital punishment and forty-three were in states with it. (The other five were in federal prisons.)

Homicide Rate Studies Have Weaknesses

All these studies have serious methodological weaknesses. One problem is the degree of comparability of states with and without the death penalty. Sellin tried to "match" states by taking contiguous ones (for example, Michigan, Indiana, and Ohio), but of course such states are not really matched at all—they differ not only in the penalty for murder but in many other respects as well, and these other differences may offset any differences resulting from the form of punishment.

Another problem lies in the definition of a capital crime. What should be studied is the rate of crimes for which capital punishment is legally possible. I am not aware of any data on "murder rates" that distinguish between those homicides (like first-degree murder) for which death may be a penalty and those (like second-degree murder or non-negligent manslaughter) for which it may not. Sellin's studies compare homicide rates, but no one knows what fraction of those homicides are first-degree murders for which execution is possible, even in the states that retain capital punishment.

Finally, and perhaps most important, it is not clear from many of these studies what is meant by "the death penalty." If what is meant is simply the legal possibility of execution, then "the death penalty" may be more fiction than fact. In many states that had the death penalty on the books, no executions were in fact carried out for many years. The majority members of a legislative commission in Massachusetts, for example, reported in 1968 that the death penalty is no deterrent to crime, but the minority members pointed out that no one had been executed in the state since 1947, and therefore no one could say whether the legal possibility of execution was or was not a deterrent. Indeed, in 1960 there were only fifty-six executions in the entire country, more than half of these occurring in the South; in 1965 there were only seven; between 1968 and 1976 there were no executions; since 1977 there have been (as of mid-1982) four.

In the same vein as Sellin's work was a study by Hans Zeisel analyzing the effects, if any, of the unofficial moratorium on executions that occurred in this country between 1968 and 1976. Zeisel argued that if executions in fact deter murders, then those states that during the late 1960s stopped executing murderers would have experienced a greater growth in the murder rate than those states that had never executed anyone for many decades. He concluded that those states that had recently stopped executions experienced less of an increase in the murder rate than did those states that had abolished capital punishment long ago. His argument was that the failure of the sudden ending of capital punishment to unleash a disproportionate increase in the murder rate was evidence that the death penalty in fact did not deter murder.

Comparative State Studies Have Weaknesses

The weakness in this argument is much the same as the weakness in the similar argument made earlier by Sellin: the states that suddenly stopped executions were very different from those that had abolished it long ago. The states that stopped in the 1960s were mostly southern states; the states that had stopped decades earlier were mostly northern states. Moreover, as Arnold Barnett has observed, massive population shifts were occurring at the same time as the changes in the death penalty, with northerners moving to the South and southerners moving to the North. These shifts may well have affected murder rates in ways that offset whatever effect the ending of capital punishment had. Finally, the states that stopped executing in the 1960s were not making much of a change in their policies, because for many years preceding the moratorium they scarcely executed anyone. Between 1960 and 1967, when they stopped, the sixteen southern states together were executing about twenty persons a year; a few individual states, such as Georgia, Florida, and Mississippi, were executing as many as two a year; most other southern states were executing virtually no one. Thus, it is by no means clear that the "change" that occurred in 1967 was significant enough to warrant a comparison between states that did and did not make it.

In short, state-by-state comparisons are not likely to tell us much about the effect of capital punishment because the states differ in so many ways in addition to their willingness to execute. There are two statistical techniques by which this problem can be addressed. One is to compare states at one point in time in ways that hold constant those social and economic factors that might influence the murder rate; the other is to analyze changes over time in the murder rate in one or more states or the nation as a whole. The first method is called "cross-sectional" analysis, the latter "longitudinal" analysis.

Cross-Sectional Studies

There have been several cross-sectional studies. One by Isaac Ehrlich, comparing states as of 1940, found that (other things being equal) executions deter homicides, and another, by Dale Cloninger, comparing states as of 1960, agreed. But other cross-sectional studies have found no deterrent effect. These include one by Peter Passell that compared states in both 1950 and 1960 and one by Brian Forst that analyzed changes across states between 1960 and 1970. There have been some lively exchanges among the authors of these studies, and a number of critics have pointed out what they believe are flaws in both the studies finding and those not finding a deterrent effect of the death penalty.

There are many reasons why these cross-sectional studies are in conflict. They often use data from different years (1940, 1950, and 1960), and it is possible the death penalty was a deterrent in some periods but not in others. They control, statistically, for somewhat different factors, and this affects the reliability with which the effect of executions is estimated. For example, Cloninger, who found that executions deter homicides, omitted from his analysis the probability of being convicted for homicide and the length of the prison terms to which nonexecuted murderers were sentenced. It is possible that some of the deterrent effect Cloninger ascribed to differences in the number of executions were in fact attributable to differences among the states in the chances of being convicted and the length of time those convicted served in prison.

Longitudinal Studies

The best-known studies attempting to discover whether executions deter murders are the longitudinal ones. Their fame rests in part on the fact that one of them, that by Isaac Ehrlich, was introduced in evidence by the Department of Justice when its lawyers were arguing in favor of the death penalty before the Supreme Court. Ehrlich's study, the first sophisticated longitudinal analysis of the death penalty, was an effort to discover what effect year-to-year changes in the number of persons executed in the United States as a whole may have had on the number of homicides committed in the nation between 1933 and 1969. He held constant changes in such social factors as the unemployment rate, labor force participation, income, and the racial and age composition of the population. He also inserted into his equation variables designed to measure the probability of a murderer being arrested and the probability of an arrested murderer being convicted. He found that changes in the probability of being executed did have an independent effect on the murder rate, as follows: every additional execution per year resulted in seven or eight fewer murders.

Kenneth I. Wolpin performed a similar analysis for England and Wales between 1929 and 1968. He concluded that, provided certain assumptions are satisfied, executing an additional murderer in a given year would produce about four fewer murder victims.

Criticism of Cross-Sectional and Longitudinal Studies

Both studies, but especially Ehrlich's, have been criticized. One criticism has to do with the assumed independence of a jury's decision to convict a charged murderer and a judge's willingness to sentence him to death. Both Ehrlich and Wolpin discovered that the higher the probability of being convicted for murder, other things being equal, the lower the murder rate, whether or not the person was executed. The implication is that convicting an alleged murderer has some deterrent effect on would-be murderers, as does executing murderers. Both propositions support the general theory of deterrence. But in the case of capital murder, they may well confound one another. Suppose a jury knew that if it found a person guilty, the chances of his being executed were very high. Common sense tells us that this knowledge would make many juries reluctant to convict some persons of first-degree murder. As a result, a greater use of executions for murder might have the effect of producing fewer convictions for murder, so that the deterrent effect of both convictions and executions would be lost. This is no mere speculative possibility. In Great Britain, where judges had less discretion in imposing death sentences than did American judges, the number of murderers found to be insane, and thus spared the gallows, dropped sharply after the death penalty was abolished in 1965. It is hard to attribute this change to a sudden improvement in the mental health of English criminals. What apparently happened was that the high probability of execution before 1965 had produced an artificially low rate of "conviction" during that period, with the insanity plea being used to avoid conviction.

Ehrlich's own data, in the opinion of some, support the conclusion that an increase in the use of the death penalty would decrease the chances of an accused murderer being convicted by about 17 percent. Such a decrease might well nullify the deterrent effect of the death penalty. Wolpin in his analysis of the English data makes it clear that in order to draw any policy conclusions from the statistical relationship between executions and murderers, one must first be confident that changing the execution rate will not change the conviction rate.

A second criticism has to do with the time period covered by the analysis. Ehrlich's study covered the years 1933 through 1969. Between 1962 and 1969, the number of executions dropped sharply, from forty-seven in 1962 to two in 1967 and zero in 1968 and 1969. And during the 1960s, crime rates, including the murder rate, were going up sharply. Suppose we omit from Ehrlich's analysis these last four years and recalculate his equations for the period 1933–1962, the period during which executions were still being used with some frequency. When Peter Passell and John B. Taylor did this, they discovered that the death penalty lost its deterrent effect, or more precisely that the statistically significant negative correlation between murders and executions disappeared. This suggests that executions were not a deterrent when they were relatively commonplace (that is, between 1933 and 1962), and the murder rate was relatively steady, but appeared to become a deterrent only after 1962, when executions decreased sharply and the murder rate rose dramatically.

But so many things were happening during the 1960s not captured in the Ehrlich equation—the increase in the private ownership of handguns, the rise in racial tensions, the growth in all forms of crime, the spread of the ethos of individual self-expression—that we cannot be confident that a finding that executions deter murder only during such unusual and brief periods warrants much confidence.

One thing in particular that was changing during the 1960s was the decline in the use of prisons and the shortening of prison sentences. While the crime rate was going up, the prison population was going down. Indeed, at all points, the criminal justice system was becoming less effective so that the chances of a given felon evading arrest, prosecution, and punishment steadily improved. These changes, more than changes in the probability of being executed (which, by 1965, was an exceedingly unlikely event in any case), may have contributed to an increase in all forms of crime, including murder.

Ehrlich did not include in his study a measure of the length of a prison sentence for murder for the very good reason that these data did not exist. But there is reason to believe that sentences were getting shorter during the 1960s. In 1960, 47 percent of the murderers released from prison had served five years or more; by 1970, only 36 percent had served terms of at least five years. If we wanted to determine the marginal deterrent effect of the death penalty, we would first find out what the effect on the murder rate would have been if prison terms had been getting longer (rather than shorter); we would then ask whether the death penalty added anything to the deterrent effect of prison.

Wolpin's study avoids some of these problems, but not all. In particular, the apparent deterrent effect of capital punishment in England and Wales, unlike that in the United States, is more or less steady over the entire period studied (1929–1968). Even though executions in England became much less common after 1957 (they were abolished a decade later), Wolpin's data suggest that the deterrent effect of executions can be detected in both the pre-1957 and post-1957 periods. On the other hand, Wolpin is not able to rule out the possibility that some of the increase in homicides that occurred, especially after World War II, was the result of a decline in the length of time served in prison by those murderers who were not executed (the English records contain no information on time served). . . .

It is possible that no statistical study, however carefully done, can shed much light on the deterrent effect of the death penalty, at least in nations that will make, at most, sparing and highly selective use of it.

Arnold Barnett has performed some calculations to show just how difficult shedding this light may be. He reviewed both cross-sectional studies finding a deterrent effect (Ehrlich) and those not finding it (Passell and Forst) and concluded that all three studies had a common problem: there was so much statistical "noise" in the analyses that it would be almost impossible to get any reliable estimates of deterrence out of them. The source of this noise is not entirely clear, but its effect is that the equations used to explain the number of executions in each state in a given year produce so many errors (that is, the difference between the predicted number of executions and the actual number occurring is so great) that the effect on murder of a rare event such as an execution could literally be swamped by the errors. For example, Passell's study led to an estimate of the total number of homicides in forty-three states in 1960 that was wrong by 1,635. If we assume that each execution might prevent five murders and since we know there were forty-four persons executed for murder in 1960, there might have been 220 murders prevented. But 220 is less than 14 percent of the 1,635 errors produced by the Passell equation. As a result, if there were a deterrent effect, Passell probably could not have found it.

Matters get worse when we recall that the vast majority of murderers would not be eligible for capital punishment in any event. Most people, I suspect, would restrict the death penalty to "cold-blooded" killers and not extend it to persons who commit crimes of passion or otherwise act impulsively. In most people's view cold-blooded killers probably include persons who deliberately murder for material gain, terrorists who kill innocent people for some political purpose, wanton murderers who derive pleasure from the act of killing, and possibly also those robbers and arsonists who carry out crimes in ways knowingly designed to cause the death of innocent bystanders. We do not know how many such murderers there are, but they undoubtedly account for only a minority, perhaps a small minority, of all homicides. For all the reasons mentioned, there will probably never be any evidence to show whether the death penalty does or does not affect the frequency with which such persons kill. If the public and elected officials are to make decisions in this matter, they will have to rely on their own best judgment. "Best judgment" means two things: a guess as to how a small number of potential offenders will react to the risk of death, and sober reflection on whether such a penalty is fair and just. Social science can contribute little to these judgments except to make clear that there is no systematic, accepted evidence that, lumping all murders together in the nation (or a state) as a whole, a change in the (small and delayed) risk of execution has a demonstrable effect on the rate at which these murders occur.

THE
HISTORY
OF
ISSUES

CHAPTER 3

Fairness and the Death Penalty

Chapter Preface

The issue of the fairness of the death penalty has been a central debate in the United States since the last century. Some of the key aspects of this debate include racial discrimination in death penalty sentences, the danger of convicting innocent defendants, and a possible bias in sparing women from death sentences.

Opponents of the death penalty have often argued that African Americans have been grossly discriminated against by the American justice system and have in many cases received unfair death sentences. In its landmark ruling in *McCleskey v. Kemp* in 1987, the U.S. Supreme Court examined such issues as race and fairness. In this case, the African American defendant Warren McCleskey was convicted of murdering a white police officer. In appealing his conviction to the Supreme Court, the defense attorney cited the findings of a study conducted by David C. Baldus. The Baldus study had concluded that black defendants accused of capital crimes were more likely to receive capital punishment than white defendants and that a sentence of death was more likely when the defendant was black and the victim was white. In other words, the defense argued that the unfair racial treatment accorded black defendants accused of capital offenses was a violation of the Fourteenth Amendment's equal protection clause and asked the Court to reverse the defendant's conviction. In its 1987 decision, the Supreme Court concluded that definite proof of racial discrimination must be offered in each individual case and that the results of the Baldus study could not be used to uphold a claim of an equal protection violation.

Of course, that decision did not quell concerns regarding fairness and race. Concerned about the fairness of the application of the death penalty in Maryland, Governor Parris Glendening issued a moratorium in 2002 on all executions in the state until the University of Maryland completes an intensive study of six thousand homicide cases to determine if the state justice system is riddled with racial and geographical bias.

Another issue crucial to a discussion of fairness and the death penalty is the risk of executing an innocent person. Opponents of capital punishment believe that this danger is reason enough to ban the death penalty. However, those in favor of capital punishment argue that the use of DNA evidence now guarantees that death sentences are fairly imposed because such incontrovertible evidence will assure that only the guilty will be executed.

A third issue central to the fairness debate is the execution of women. Although women have been executed in the United States since colonial times, they have been executed in much smaller numbers than men—a disproportion that some argue is the result of gender bias in favor of women. Citing the unfairness of this apparent bias, attorney and professor Elizabeth Rapaport seeks gender "equality of the damned." She predicts that in the near future, such equality will assure that when women are found guilty of capital crimes, their gender will not impede the execution process.

These issues and others concerning the fairness of capital punishment continue to fuel the national debate. In the following chapter, the authors examine some of the arguments that have been made about the fairness of this practice.

Racial Discrimination in Death Penalty Sentences Must Be Proved on a Case-by-Case Basis

LEWIS F. POWELL

University of Iowa professor David C. Baldus conducted a study of more than two thousand Georgia murder cases that took place during a five-year period in the 1970s. Baldus concluded that black defendants (accused of murder) were more likely to receive capital punishment than white defendants. The research also showed that a sentence of death was even more likely when the defendant was black and the victim was white. The Baldus study became the central defense in a case in 1978. On October 12 of that year, Warren McCleskey was convicted of murder and armed robbery and sentenced to death in the electric chair by a jury in the Superior Court of Fulton County, Georgia. McCleskey was black and the murder victim, a police officer, was white. The case excerpts that follow describe the arguments made by the McCleskey defense before the Supreme Court and the Court's ruling in McCleskey's appeal of his conviction. Citing the Baldus study,

Lewis F. Powell, opinion, *McCleskey v. Kemp*, U.S. Supreme Court, 1987.

the McCleskey defense first argues that his death sentence is unconstitutional under the Fourteenth Amendment's equal protection clause because he was discriminated against as a black defendant with a white victim. Moreover, again citing the Baldus findings, the defense argues that his death sentence was unconstitutional under the Eighth Amendment's cruel and unusual punishment clause because the racial factors in his sentencing rendered the punishment arbitrary. Writing for the Court, Justice Lewis F. Powell first considers the Fourteenth Amendment and the equal protection clause. Powell concludes that definite proof of discrimination—not just the results of the Baldus study—must be offered in McCleskey's individual case to uphold a claim of an equal protection violation. In considering the Eighth Amendment claim, Powell concludes that the death sentence was rendered in accordance with Georgia law and was not arbitrarily imposed. Justice Lewis F. Powell, nominated by President Richard M. Nixon, served on the U.S. Supreme Court from 1971 to 1987. He cast the deciding vote in many death penalty decisions.

This case presents the question whether a complex statistical study that indicates a risk that racial considerations enter into capital sentencing determinations proves that petitioner McCleskey's capital sentence is unconstitutional under the Eighth or Fourteenth Amendment.

McCleskey, a black man, was convicted of two counts of armed robbery and one count of murder in the Superior Court of Fulton County, Georgia, on October 12, 1978. McCleskey's convictions arose out of the robbery of a furniture store and the killing of a white police officer during the course of the robbery. . . .

The Baldus Study

In support of his claim, McCleskey proffered a statistical study performed by Professors David C. Baldus, Charles Pulaski, and George Woodworth (the Baldus study), that purports to show a disparity in the imposition of the death sentence in Georgia based on the race of the murder victim and, to a lesser extent, the race of the defendant. The Baldus study is actually two sophisticated statistical studies that examine over 2,000 murder cases that occurred in Georgia during the 1970's. The raw numbers collected by Professor Baldus indicate that defendants charged with killing white persons received the death penalty in 11 percent of the cases, but defendants charged with killing blacks received the death penalty in only 1 percent of the cases. The raw numbers also indicate a reverse racial disparity according to the race of the defendant: 4 percent of the black defendants received the death penalty, as opposed to 7 percent of the white defendants.

Baldus also divided the cases according to the combination of the race of the defendant and the race of the victim. He found that the death penalty was assessed in 22 percent of the cases involving black defendants and white victims; 8 percent of the cases involving white defendants and white victims; 1 percent of the cases involving black defendants and black victims; and 3 percent of the cases involving white defendants and black victims. Similarly, Baldus found that prosecutors sought the death penalty in 70 percent of the cases involving black defendants and white victims; 32 percent of the cases involving white defendants and white victims; 15 percent of the cases involving black defendants and black victims; and 19 percent of the cases involving white defendants and black victims.

Baldus subjected his data to an extensive analysis, taking account of 230 variables that could have explained the disparities on nonracial grounds. One of his models concludes that, even after taking account of 39 nonracial variables, defendants charged with killing white victims were 4.3 times as likely to receive a death sentence as defendants charged with killing blacks. According to this model, black defendants were 1.1 times as likely to receive a death sentence as other defendants. Thus, the Baldus study indicates that black defendants, such as McCleskey, who kill white victims have the greatest likelihood of receiving the death penalty. . . .

Race and Equal Protection

McCleskey's first claim is that the Georgia capital punishment statute violates the Equal Protection Clause of the Fourteenth Amendment. He argues that race has infected the administration of Georgia's statute in two ways: persons who murder whites are more likely to be sentenced to death than persons who murder blacks, and black murderers are more likely to be sentenced to death than white murderers. As a black defendant who killed a white victim, McCleskey claims that the Baldus study demonstrates that he was discriminated against because of his race and because of the race of his victim. In its broadest form, McCleskey's claim of discrimination extends to every actor in the Georgia capital sentencing process, from the prosecutor who sought the death penalty and the jury that imposed the sentence, to the State itself that enacted the capital punishment statute and allows it to remain in effect despite its allegedly discriminatory application. We agree with the Court of Appeals, and every other court that has considered such a challenge, that this claim must fail.

Proving Discrimination

Our analysis begins with the basic principle that a defendant who alleges an equal protection violation has the burden of proving "the existence of purposeful discrimination.". . . A corollary to this principle is that a criminal defendant must prove that the purposeful discrimination "had a discriminatory effect" on him. . . . Thus, to prevail under the Equal Protection Clause, McCleskey must prove that the decisionmakers in his case acted with discriminatory purpose. He offers no evidence specific to his own case that would support an inference that racial considerations played a part in his sentence. Instead, he relies solely on the Baldus study.

McCleskey argues that the Baldus study compels an inference that his sentence rests on purposeful discrimination. McCleskey's claim that these statistics are sufficient proof of discrimination, without regard to the facts of a particular case, would extend to all capital cases in Georgia, at least where the victim was white and the defendant is black. . . .

McCleskey challenges decisions at the heart of the State's criminal justice system. "One of society's most basic tasks is that of protecting the lives of its citizens and one of the most basic ways in which it achieves the task is through criminal laws against murder." *Gregg v. Georgia* (1976). Implementation of these laws necessarily requires discretionary judgments. Because discretion is essential to the criminal justice process, we would demand exceptionally clear proof before we would infer that the discretion has been abused. The unique nature of the decisions at issue in this case also counsels against adopting such an inference from the disparities indicated by the Baldus study. Accordingly, we hold that the Baldus study is clearly insufficient to support an inference that any of the decisionmakers in McCleskey's case acted with discriminatory purpose.

McCleskey also suggests that the Baldus study proves that the State as a whole has acted with a discriminatory purpose. He appears to argue that the State has violated the Equal Protection Clause by adopting the capital punishment statute and allowing it to remain in force despite its allegedly discriminatory application. But "'discriminatory purpose' . . . implies more than intent as volition or intent as awareness of consequences. It implies that the decisionmaker, in this case a state legislature, selected or reaffirmed a particular course of action at least in part 'because of,' not merely 'in spite of,' its adverse effects upon an identifiable group.". . . For this claim to prevail, McCleskey would have to prove that the Georgia Legislature enacted or maintained the death penalty statute because of an anticipated racially discriminatory effect. In *Gregg v. Georgia*, this Court found that the Georgia capital sentencing system could operate in a fair and neutral manner. There was no evidence then, and there is none now, that the Georgia Legislature enacted the capital punishment statute to further a racially discriminatory purpose.

Nor has McCleskey demonstrated that the legislature maintains the capital punishment statute because of the racially disproportionate impact suggested by the Baldus study. As legislatures necessarily have wide discretion in the choice of criminal laws and penalties, and as there were legitimate reasons for the Georgia Legislature to adopt and maintain capital punishment, see *Gregg*, we will not infer a discriminatory purpose on the part of the State of Georgia. Accordingly, we reject McCleskey's equal protection claims.

Sentencing Related to the Crime

McCleskey also argues that the Baldus study demonstrates that the Georgia capital sentencing system violates the Eighth Amendment. . . .

In light of our precedents under the Eighth Amendment, McCleskey cannot argue successfully that his sentence is "disproportionate to the crime in the traditional sense." He does not deny that he committed a murder in the course of a planned robbery, a crime for which this Court has determined that the death penalty constitutionally may be imposed. His disproportionality claim "is of a different sort." *Gregg v. Georgia* (1976). McCleskey argues that the sentence in his case is disproportionate to the sentences in other murder cases.

On the one hand, he cannot base a constitutional claim on an argument that his case differs from other cases in which defendants did receive the death penalty. On automatic appeal, the Georgia Supreme Court found that McCleskey's death sentence was not disproportionate to other death sentences imposed in the State. . . . The court supported this conclusion with an appendix containing citations to 13 cases involving generally similar murders. . . . Moreover, where the statutory procedures adequately channel the sentencer's discretion, such proportionality review is not constitutionally required.

On the other hand, absent a showing that the Georgia capital punishment system operates in an arbitrary and capricious manner, McCleskey cannot prove a constitutional violation by demonstrating that other defendants who may be similarly situated did not receive the death penalty. . . .

Because McCleskey's sentence was imposed under Georgia sentencing procedures that focus discretion "on the particularized nature of the crime and the particularized characteristics of the individual defendant," . . . we lawfully may presume that McCleskey's death sentence was not "wantonly and freakishly" imposed, . . . and thus that the sentence is not disproportionate within any recognized meaning under the Eighth Amendment.

Racial Prejudice and Sentencing

Although our decision in *Gregg* as to the facial validity of the Georgia capital punishment statute appears to foreclose McCleskey's disproportionality argument, he further contends that the Georgia capital punishment system is arbitrary and capricious in application, and therefore his sentence is excessive, because racial considerations may influence capital sentencing decisions in Georgia. We now address this claim.

To evaluate McCleskey's challenge, we must examine exactly what the Baldus study may show. Even Professor Baldus does not contend that his statistics prove that race enters into any capital sentencing decisions or that race was a factor in McCleskey's particular case. Statistics at most may show only a likelihood that a particular factor entered into some decisions. There is, of course, some risk of racial prejudice influencing a jury's decision in a criminal case. There are similar risks that other kinds of prejudice will influence other criminal trials. The question "is at what point that risk becomes constitutionally unacceptable." *Turner v. Murray* (1986). McCleskey asks us to accept the likelihood allegedly shown by the Baldus study as the constitutional measure of an unacceptable risk of racial prejudice influencing capital sentencing decisions. This we decline to do.

Because of the risk that the factor of race may enter the criminal justice process, we have engaged in "unceasing efforts" to eradicate racial prejudice from our criminal justice system. . . . Our efforts have been guided by our recognition that "the inestimable privilege of trial by jury . . . is a vital principle, underlying the whole administration of criminal justice.". . . Thus, it is the jury that is a criminal defendant's fundamental "protection of life and liberty against race or color prejudice.". . . Specifically, a capital sentencing jury representative of a criminal defendant's community assures a "'diffused impartiality,'" . . . in the jury's task of "express[ing] the conscience of the community on the ultimate question of life or death." *Witherspoon v. Illinois* (1968).

Individual jurors bring to their deliberations "qualities of human nature and varieties of human experience, the range of which is unknown and perhaps unknowable.". . . The capital sentencing decision requires the individual jurors to focus their collective judgment on the unique characteristics of a particular criminal defendant. It is not surprising that such collective judgments often are difficult to explain. But the inherent lack of predictability of jury decisions does not justify their condemnation. On the contrary, it is the jury's function to make the difficult and uniquely human judgments that defy codification and that "build discretion, equity, and flexibility into a legal system." H. Kalven and H. Zeisel, The American Jury 498 (1966).

McCleskey's argument that the Constitution condemns the discretion allowed decisionmakers in the Georgia capital sentencing system is antithetical to the fundamental role of discretion in our criminal justice system. Discretion in the criminal justice system offers substantial benefits to the criminal defendant. Not only can a jury decline to impose the death sentence, it can decline to convict or choose to convict of a lesser offense. Whereas decisions against a defendant's interest may be reversed by the trial judge or on appeal, these discretionary exercises of leniency are final and unreviewable. Similarly, the capacity of prosecutorial discretion to provide individualized justice is "firmly entrenched in American law.". . . As we have noted, a prosecutor can decline to charge, offer a plea bargain, or decline to seek a death sentence in any particular case. . . . Of course, "the power to be lenient [also] is the power to discriminate," . . . but a capital punishment system that did not allow for discretionary acts of leniency "would be totally alien to our notions of criminal justice.". . .

Racial Bias and McCleskey Sentencing

At most, the Baldus study indicates a discrepancy that appears to correlate with race. Apparent disparities in sentencing are an inevitable part of our criminal justice system. The discrepancy indicated by the Baldus study is "a far cry from the major systemic defects identified in *Furman* [*v. Georgia*, a 1972 case in which death penalty statutes were ruled unconstitutional]." *Pulley v. Harris* (1984). As this Court has recognized, any mode for determining guilt or punishment "has its weaknesses and the potential for misuse.". . . Specifically, "there can be 'no perfect procedure for deciding in which cases governmental authority should be used to impose death.'" . . . Despite these imperfections, our consistent rule has been that constitutional guarantees are met when "the mode [for determining guilt or punishment] itself has been surrounded with safeguards to make it as fair as possible.". . . Where the discretion that is fundamental to our criminal process is involved, we decline to assume that what is unexplained is invidious. In light of the safeguards designed to minimize racial bias in the process, the fundamental value of jury trial in our criminal justice system, and the benefits that discretion provide to criminal defendants, we hold that the Baldus study does not demonstrate a constitutionally significant risk of racial bias affecting the Georgia capital sentencing process.

Two additional concerns inform our decision in this case. First, McCleskey's claim, taken to its logical conclusion, throws into serious question the principles that underlie our entire criminal justice system. The Eighth Amendment is not limited in application to capital punishment, but applies to all penalties. Thus, if we accepted McCleskey's claim that racial bias has impermissibly tainted the capital sentencing decision, we could soon be faced with similar claims as to other types of penalty. Moreover, the claim that his sentence rests on the irrelevant factor of race easily could be extended to apply to claims based on unexplained discrepancies that correlate to membership in other minority groups, and even to gender. Similarly, since McCleskey's claim relates to the race of his victim, other claims could apply with equally logical force to statistical disparities that correlate with the race or sex of other actors in the criminal justice system, such as defense attorneys or judges. Also, there is no logical reason that such a claim need be limited to racial or sexual bias. If arbitrary and capricious punishment is the touchstone under the Eighth Amendment, such a claim could—at least in theory—be based upon any arbitrary variable, such as the defendant's facial characteristics, or the physical attractiveness of the defendant or the victim, that some statistical study indicates may be influential in jury decisionmaking. As these examples illustrate, there is no limiting principle to the type of challenge brought by McCleskey. The Constitution does not require that a State eliminate any demonstrable disparity that correlates with a potentially irrelevant factor in order to operate a criminal justice system that includes capital punishment. As we have stated specifically in the context of capital punishment, the Constitution does not "place totally unrealistic conditions on its use." *Gregg v. Georgia* (1976).

Second, McCleskey's arguments are best presented to the legislative bodies. It is not the responsibility—or indeed even the right—of this Court to determine the appropriate punishment for particular crimes. It is the legislatures, the elected representatives of the people, that are "constituted to respond to the will and consequently the moral values of the people." *Furman v. Georgia*, 408 U.S., at 383 (Burger, C.J., dissenting). Legislatures also are better qualified to weigh and "evaluate the results of statistical studies in terms of their own local conditions and with a flexibility of approach that is not available to the courts." *Gregg v. Georgia* (1976). Capital punishment is now the law in more than two-thirds of our States. It is the ultimate duty of courts to determine on a case-by-case basis whether these laws are applied consistently with the Constitution. Despite McCleskey's wide-ranging arguments that basically challenge the validity of capital punishment in our multiracial society, the only question before us is whether in his case, the law of Georgia was properly applied. We agree with the District Court and the Court of Appeals for the Eleventh Circuit that this was carefully and correctly done in this case.

Many People Have Been Wrongfully Sentenced to Death in New York

MARTY I. ROSENBAUM

The New York State Defenders Association (a group of lawyers who specialize in representing people accused of crimes) examined a number of capital murder cases that occurred in that state from 1965 to 1988 in which the accused murderer was convicted in error. The following selection is an excerpt from the study, written by Marty I. Rosenbaum of the Office of Program and Counsel for the New York State Assembly. Rosenbaum briefly describes the history of the death penalty in New York State and points out that New York has sentenced more innocent persons to death than any other state except Florida. He then lists some of the factors that contribute to such a high degree of error: prosecutorial misconduct, witness error, perjury (lying under oath), unreliable circumstantial evidence, and incompetent counsel for the accused. Rosenbaum also describes numerous New York murder cases in which the accused was convicted and later found innocent. He concludes by stating the Defenders Association's position that innocent defendants will inevitably be convicted and executed if the state of New York reinstates its capital punishment laws. (New York reinstated its death penalty statute in 1995.)

Marty I. Rosenbaum, "The Inevitable Error: Wrongful New York State Homicide Convictions, 1965–1988," *New York University Review of Law and Social Change*, vol. XVIII, 1990–1991, pp. 807–30. Copyright © 1991 by Marty I. Rosenbaum. Reproduced by permission.

This Article reports the preliminary results of a continuing study by the New York State Defenders Association's Wrongful Conviction Study Project. The purpose of the study is to catalogue wrongful homicide convictions in New York State during the period from 1965 to 1988. The Project has found a significant number of wrongful convictions, as defined and reported below. The data presented in this Article support the position that the State of New York should not reenact the death penalty. If New York does so, the Association's study suggests, there will almost certainly be a significant number of persons wrongfully convicted of capital murder in New York, and many of these persons will very possibly be executed before the errors are discovered, if they are discovered at all. Stated simply, the study indicates the fallibility of the New York criminal justice system, which militates against the use of capital punishment.

The Association has defined the subject of its study as follows: a "wrongful homicide conviction" is a conviction for any degree of homicide—including murder, manslaughter, or criminally negligent homicide—which is overturned and never reinstated. This includes basically three categories of cases: those where the conviction was overturned and either (a) the defendant was subsequently acquitted on retrial (seventeen of the cases catalogued below), (b) the charges were dismissed (thirty-five cases), or (c) the charges were resolved by conviction of a non-homicide crime (seven cases, of which three also included acquittals on the homicide charges). There is no subjective element whatsoever to the study: it merely catalogues the cases which fit the above definition.

The study has thus far found fifty-nine such cases during the twenty-three-year period reviewed, each of which is separately noted below. These findings in no way purport to be exhaustive, and the author is reviewing additional cases which may eventually supplement those listed here.

History of the Death Penalty in New York

The death penalty has a long history in New York State. New York was the first state to employ the electric chair as a method of execution, a practice which led to one of the United States Supreme Court's earliest decisions on capital punishment. Although death penalty legislation has remained on the books in New York throughout the twentieth century, the last person to be executed in the state was Eddie Lee Mays, in 1963. Following the United States Supreme Court's decision in *Woodson v. North Carolina*, the New York Court of Appeals has held that the mandatory nature of the New York death penalty statute violates the United States Constitution. The decisions of the Court of Appeals have left in place only a very limited provision in the statute for those who murder a police officer, but this mandatory death penalty provision is clearly unconstitutional in view of these Court of Appeals decisions and the United States Supreme Court's decision in *Sumner v. Schuman* [a 1987 case that ruled that a mandatory death sentence for a murder committed by a prisoner who is serving a life sentence is unconstitutional]. Although there have been repeated attempts to enact a new and expanded death penalty statute in New York, those attempts have failed due to executive vetoes.

During the period from 1900 to 1985, New York is estimated to have sentenced more innocent persons to death than any other state in the country except Florida. New York has the dubious distinction of leading all states in executing the innocent; eight New Yorkers have been executed in error. During recent years, this issue has continued to haunt the state, as the question of erroneous convictions has been central to the debate over whether to reenact the death penalty in New York. Governor Mario M. Cuomo, members of the State Senate and Assembly, the news media and others have stressed the imperfection of the criminal justice system and the potential for a miscarriage of justice as one of the most important reasons not to enact death penalty legislation. The results of the Association's study support this position.

Reasons for Errors

Several important points regarding erroneous convictions should be made before presenting the raw data. First, a substantial number of the wrongful convictions we have found in New York resulted from prosecutorial misconduct. Such misconduct has included, among other things, the suppression of exculpatory evidence and the conscious use of perjured testimony. There is no reason to believe that prosecutorial misconduct would be any less prevalent in capital cases. Indeed, given the generally high public profile of capital cases, which often involve brutal deaths that have inflamed the community, the likelihood of prosecutorial overzealousness and misconduct is arguably enhanced in cases where the death penalty is sought. This suggestion is supported by the fact that prosecutorial misconduct has been shown to have resulted in wrongful convictions in death penalty cases in a number of other states in recent years.

Besides prosecutorial misconduct, police misconduct can also contribute to an erroneous conviction. Police may suppress evidence, coerce false confessions, or simply conduct negligent investigations. Like prosecutorial misconduct, there is no reason to believe that this type of misconduct occurs to any lesser degree in capital cases, and some reason to believe that it may occur to an even greater degree.

Wrongful convictions also result from other factors. For example, witness error is a significant factor in erroneous judgments, and may arise from mistaken eyewitness identification, perjury by a witness, or simply unreliable prosecution testimony. In addition, misleading circumstantial evidence, incompetence of defense counsel, erroneous judgment as to a cause of death, and a variety of other factors can lead to a conviction that is rendered in error.

Finally, it should be noted that in many of the cases we have studied, the defendant was exonerated only after having spent many years in prison. Often the direct appeals process had been exhausted and only the persistence of a family member, a friend, the defendant pro se, or a volunteer led to the discovery of exculpatory evidence and the defendant's release. This illustrates not only the fundamental unfairness that results from any miscarriage of justice, but also that if capital punishment is reinstated in New York, there is a substantial likelihood that death sentences will be carried out before errors are revealed.

Summary of Cases

• Miguel Arroyo was convicted of manslaughter in Kings County on May 12, 1965, for killing a boy involved in a street fight outside Arroyo's store. The trial judge set aside the verdict when Arroyo's defense counsel produced a series of eyewitnesses who testified that they had seen another man, José Velasquez, kill the boy. Key witnesses who had testified against Arroyo then recanted their testimony. Velasquez was arrested and indicted for murder, and in 1966 the indictment against Arroyo was dismissed.

• Arthur Barber was convicted of first-degree murder in Bronx County on December 2, 1969, for a 1965 killing, and was sentenced to life in prison. Although all state appellate courts affirmed the conviction, the federal district court reversed it in 1975 because Barber had been arrested without probable cause, beaten by the police, and subjected to numerous other illegal police tactics in violation of his constitutional rights. The court concluded that Barber's confession had been obtained by the police through "brutal treatment" that was "so offensive as to constitute violations of Barber's constitutional right of due process." All charges were dismissed and Barber was released from prison.

• Bryan Blake was convicted of second-degree murder in New York County on December 5, 1985. The conviction was reversed on July 14, 1988, on the grounds that both defendant's videotaped statement, containing improper remarks by the prosecutor, and photographs of the victim's body, which were shown to the jury during trial, were unduly prejudicial. Blake had been sentenced to twenty-five years to life in prison. The jury which heard the case on retrial acquitted him after ninety minutes of deliberation. "It wasn't even close," said one juror. Said another: "We felt they had no case. . . . We were surprised it got to the grand jury. It's incredible what can happen to people, to be dragged into court with such a little bit of evidence." Blake had served over three years on the wrongful conviction.

• Larry Boone was convicted of murder in Bronx County on December 6, 1973. The conviction was reversed on July 15, 1975, because the prosecutor had failed to disclose crucial exculpatory evidence. On remand, the trial court dismissed all charges because the detective's notes had been lost and because witnesses favorable to the defense (whose identities were not revealed by the government at the time of trial) were no longer available, and because there was no proof of Boone's criminal intent other than his mere presence at the scene. The Court of Claims granted Boone summary judgment on his wrongful imprisonment compensation claim. He had been sentenced to twenty-five years to life in prison, and had served nearly two years before being released.

• Georgino Borrero, a store security guard, was convicted of criminally negligent homicide in Bronx County on July 6, 1983, in the shooting death of John Johnson. On appeal in 1986, the Appellate Division found that, after Johnson pulled a gun on him, Borrero had left the store to find a police officer and fired only when Johnson advanced toward him with a gun and assumed a "combat stance." The court found that Borrero had "acted entirely reasonably. . . . [His] conduct was that of a responsible citizen." His conviction was reversed and the indictment dismissed.

• Daniel P. Boutin was convicted of two counts of criminally negligent homicide in Saratoga County on February 5, 1987. While driving his truck on the Adirondack Northway in Saratoga County, Boutin collided with a police car that had stopped in the right hand roadway behind a disabled tractor trailer. The police car's lights were flashing, but visibility was low due to fog and rain. Both the state trooper and the driver of the disabled truck, who were seated inside the police vehicle, were killed. The Appellate Division affirmed the conviction, but the Court of Appeals reversed, holding that

> the evidence does not show that defendant was engaged in any criminally culpable risk-creating conduct. . . . Rather, it establishes only that defendant inexplicably failed to see the vehicle until he was so close that he could not prevent the collision. . . . That unexplained failure, without more, does not constitute criminally negligent homicide.

• José Carrasquillo was convicted of second-degree manslaughter in New York County on December 17, 1986. The prosecution charged that Carrasquillo had inflicted a fatal blow upon the victim, who was apparently shoplifting from the boutique where the defendant worked. The victim died two days after the attack. The Appellate Division reversed the conviction on April 21, 1988, and ordered the indictment dismissed. The court held that the evidence was insufficient to establish that Carrasquillo, rather than his accomplice, had struck the fatal blow.

• Nathaniel Carter was convicted of murder in the stabbing of his mother-in-law in Queens County on September 13, 1982, and was sentenced to twenty-five years to life in prison. The prosecution's star witness was the victim's daughter, Carter's estranged wife, Delissa, who testified that she had seen the defendant stab her mother. Carter continually protested his innocence. Peekskill police officer James Nelson, a childhood friend of Carter's, investigated the case and became convinced that Carter could not have been in Queens at the time of the murder. Lieutenant Nelson contacted Legal Aid lawyers, who convinced Queens District Attorney John Santucci that Carter had been wrongly convicted. Santucci then had Delissa Carter arrested as a material witness. Believing she was being arrested for the killing, Delissa Carter promptly confessed to the crime. Nathaniel Carter was released from prison on January 17, 1984, after nearly two and one-half years in prison. In 1986, Carter accepted an out-of-court settlement of $450,000 to compensate for his wrongful conviction.

• Thomas A. Cenzi was convicted of second-degree murder in Monroe County on February 27, 1980, and was sentenced to twenty years to life in prison. The trial judge improperly permitted the jury to consider an uncounseled statement taken after Cenzi's retained counsel had instructed the police not to question him. Cenzi challenged the evidentiary ruling on appeal, and the Appellate Division ordered a new trial. Cenzi was acquitted of all charges on April 11, 1983.

• Arthur Cleveland was convicted of murder in Bronx County on December 6, 1973, along with co-defendant Larry Boone, and was sentenced to twenty years to life in prison. His conviction was reversed in 1975 on the authority of *People v. Boone*, on the grounds that the prosecutor had unconstitutionally failed to disclose crucial exculpatory evidence. The trial court on remand dismissed all charges. Cleveland had been imprisoned for four and one-half years.

• Patricia Cohen was convicted of second-degree murder in Westchester County on March 2, 1979, in the shooting death of her husband, and sentenced to twenty years to life in prison. Cohen steadfastly maintained her innocence, contending that her husband had committed suicide. After an unsuccessful appeal to the Appellate Division, the Court of Appeals reversed and vacated the conviction on grounds that (1) the state's "survey" evidence concerning how far the "average" suicide victim holds the gun from his body was unreliable; and (2) results of test firings of the weapon were erroneously admitted because there was no proof the objects through which the test bullets passed possessed characteristics similar to human skin. On remand, the trial court suppressed certain evidence. The prosecutor unsuccessfully appealed the suppression ruling to the Appellate Division and Court of Appeals and unsuccessfully sought review in the United States Supreme Court. Cohen was thereafter convicted only of criminal possession of a weapon in the third degree.

• Rafael Cruz was convicted of murder in Kings County on September 8, 1986. The Appellate Division ruled that Cruz had been improperly questioned in the absence of his attorney after the commencement of a formal judicial action. The court reversed his murder conviction, ordered the statement suppressed, and remanded for a new trial. At the retrial, Cruz was acquitted of all charges.

• Melvin Dlugash was convicted of murder in Kings County in 1975 in the shooting death of Michael Geller. Dlugash acknowledged that he fired at Geller, but asserted that Geller was already dead at the time, as co-defendant Joseph Bush had fatally shot Geller several minutes earlier. Dlugash maintained that he fired because he feared Bush would harm him if he did not do so. Dlugash's murder conviction was set aside in 1977 because the prosecutor failed to establish that Geller was alive at the time Dlugash fired. In 1977, the Appellate Division substituted a verdict of attempted murder and remanded the case for resentencing.

• Vernon Ellis was convicted of first-degree manslaughter in New York County on October 1, 1976. His conviction was set aside by the Appellate Division in 1978. The appellate court reasoned that the trial judge's "excessive questioning and examination of witnesses, including the defendant . . . [made] him appear to be an advocate rather than an impartial arbiter. The prosecutor did not retry the case and Ellis was freed. He had been imprisoned for two years on the wrongful conviction. . . .

Conclusion from Case Summaries

The data presented above show that erroneous convictions occur with regularity in homicide cases in New York. Wrongful convictions will undoubtedly also occur in capital cases if New York reinstates the death penalty. Once carried out, erroneous death sentences are irreversible. Since there is an ever present risk of wrongful convictions and executions. New York should avoid enacting capital punishment legislation.

Slavery, Lynching, and the Death Penalty as Methods of Social Control

WILLIAM S. McFEELY

In this excerpt, William S. McFeely explores what he describes as the link between African Americans and the "societal infliction of death." He begins by looking at slavery in the United States and the violence associated with that institution. He then considers the role that lynching—and the threat of being lynched—played in the entrenchment of the post–Civil War Jim Crow laws in American society. McFeely portrays the proliferation of capital sentences in the United States as a direct outgrowth of the decline in the number of lynchings. Calling the death penalty a form of "legal lynching," he describes the similarities between these two forms of punishment and how they disproportionately impact poor, black citizens in the United States. McFeely is a professor emeritus in the humanities at the University of Georgia in Athens. He was awarded a Pulitzer Prize in 1982 for his book Grant: A Biography. *He is also the author of* The Black Man in the Land of Equality *and* Frederick Douglass.

There is a link between African Americans and the death penalty, or more generally, African Americans and societal infliction of death. It is necessary for us neither to count

William S. McFeely, "Capital Cases: A Legacy of Slavery and Lynching: The Death Penalty as a Tool of Social Control," *The Champion*, November 3, 1997, pp. 1–8. Reproduced by permission.

up the numbers of black Americans who have been killed nor to recount a history of racism. What is important to a discussion of the present-day death penalty, is to look at certain uses of violence over the course of American history.

The physical pain meted out under slavery and by lynchers had the purpose of creating a psychological fear designed to control a large stretch of black communities. In the past, there were two reasons for exercising that control—the need for labor and fear of the black people who were the laborers.

In the 1990s there is no longer the same need for that labor, but the fear remains. Many in the majority community, consisting of both the affluent and those afraid of slipping from economic security, dread not only black folk, but the poor in general. Desperate poverty may lead to desperate acts, thus, those who feel threatened by this desperation use the power of the state to control those they fear. To exercise that control, there are increasing calls for and use of the death penalty.

Slavery in the United States

Slavery in the United States was an immensely complex system. Crucial to its maintenance was the threat, often carried out, of the pain of the whip, the anguish of forced separations by sale, and the finality of death. Frederick Douglass recalled from his childhood the shooting of a slave named Demby by Austin Gore, an overseer on the huge farm on which Douglass (then Frederick Bailey) lived.

Douglass remembered the scene of Gore taking up a whip: "He had given Demby but few stripes, when to get rid of the scourging, he [Demby] plunged himself into a creek, and stood there at the depth of his shoulders, refusing to come out. Mr. Gore told him that he would give him three calls, and that, if he did not come out at the third call, he would shoot him. The first call was given. Demby made no response, but stood his ground. The second and third calls were given with the same result. Mr. Gore then . . . raised his musket to his face . . . , taking deadly aim . . . , and in an instant poor Demby was no more. His mangled body sank out of sight, and blood and brains marked the water where he had stood.". . .

The Gore story might make people assume that the slavery period presented the greatest threat to African American lives. We prefer to think that the worst of times were in the past. To be sure, there were examples of cold-blooded murder, as in the instance of Gore, or when a master, in moments of frustration, fear of his slaves, and rage, whipped a slave to death or shot him or her. There were, however, several constraints. In the first place a slave was property worth a lot of money. In addition, social pressure sometimes operated to repress the grossest of mistreatment. An owner who mistreated "his people" might be shunned by his neighbors. Rarely, there was even access to the courts. A North Carolina slave owner was tried and convicted for the torture-murder of a slave woman. Even the insurrectionary, Nat Turner, was accorded a trial.

But Turner, a free black preacher who, in 1831, led the most famous slave revolt, was executed in a horrible fashion. The revolt not only brought an end to any Southern plans for gradual emancipation such as those the Virginia legislature was about to debate, but also led to the tightening of the Southern white resolve to impose more severe control over their slaves and to defy any Northern efforts to end slavery. Most slaves were left with a sense of the uselessness of any direct challenge to that control.

There were white people in authority who did consider the welfare of individual slaves. Frederick Douglass, after a failed attempt at escape, was spared a lynching or being sold South by his owner, Thomas Auld. Instead, Auld sent the slave to his brother in Baltimore. There, as Auld must have expected, Douglass attempted escape again, this time successfully.

During Reconstruction, following the Civil War, champions different from patriarchal masters appeared. These were Federal District Judges and an Attorney General of the United States who thought the Civil War really had been about something and undertook to enforce the Thirteenth and Fourteenth Amendments to the Constitution. In 1867, Chief Justice Salmon P. Chase ruled that an involuntary apprenticeship law in Maryland constituted a return of slavery and was in violation of the Thirteenth Amendment. In 1871 Attorney General Amos Akerman, an ex-Confederate officer from Georgia, using the power of the newly created Justice Department, sent federal marshals into South Carolina to round up murderous Klansmen who were thwarting the political and economic assertions of the freed people. Indictments were obtained and the perpetrators of outlaw killings were brought before federal judges for violation of the Fourteenth Amendment. Intimidation of witnesses made convictions scant, but the power of the Klan was seriously curtailed. . . .

In the 1880s black farmers gathered a measure of power by banding together in the Colored Farmers' Alliances to address the problems of rural poverty. Later, they formed an uneasy link with the radical People's Party. This genuine threat to the power of the landowning establishment was met not only by shrewd political maneuvering, but also by lynchings, used increasingly to reassert white social control.

Indeed, by the close of the nineteenth century and well into the twentieth, lynching, disenfranchisement, and the formal categorization of Negroes as separate of the Jim Crow laws caused African Americans to be as powerless in America as they had ever been. Such humiliations as separate drinking fountains were part of the wall deliberately erected between Americans. Not even under slavery had African Americans been so excluded from any recourse to those in authority.

Death Penalty and the Legal System

Is there a link between "lynch law" and statutory capital punishment law, between torture, mutilation, and death on a tree outside town and the orderly procedure of placing a person in a chair and throwing a switch, or, more antiseptically, on a gurney and injecting a needle within legal walls? Is the death penalty a direct descendant of lynching?

The merger of the two is the phenomenon known as legal lynching. As killings outside the law declined in the twentieth-century South, the infliction of the death penalty by the courts increased. The hundred-a-year lynchings of the 1890s were matched by similar numbers of legal executions in the 1930s. (This year [1997] Texas may top the record it set in the 1930s.) Critics coined the phrase "legal lynching.". . .

The scholar who has done the most sophisticated work on lynching, Fitzhugh Brundage—studying, county by county, where killings did and did not occur and why—is uncomfortable with what he sees as a glib connection between lynching and legal lynching. Brundage is not so sure that the courts were ready to do the lynchers work. He points to judges in the nineteenth century who, far from agreeing to do the lynchers work for them, genuinely tried to provide a fair trial for a defendant. Brundage also points out the irony that this admirable approach often enraged a community and provoked a lynching.

The political implication of Brundage's cautionary approach is that we should not tear up the criminal justice system, root and branch. Some scholars come close to urging a radical change in the system that would require such yanking. They may be right. But don't hold your breath. For worse rather than better, we have our legal system.

When we look at what does exist, can we sometimes see a link between death at the close of a legal lynching and the same result after turning to the supposedly safeguarding procedures established post-*Furman* [the 1972 case in which the U.S. Supreme Court ruled the death penalty unconstitutional] by legislatures? Are we not seeing eager prosecutors and judges up for election achieving death sentences almost as trophies? How effective is the automatic review? Even if relief is granted, with no right to counsel, who is to defend the indigent at subsequent appearances in court? If someone steps in to appeal, are there not limitations to the process that almost insure a death?

What is more, isn't the actuality of one man's death as retribution, a deliberate threat to a whole community? Individual black criminals are not deterred from further violent crimes, but a controlling pall does fall over an African American community.

The Brundage challenge to the link between lynching and the death penalty, if technically correct, misses the psychological connection between lynching, legal lynching, and the present-day death penalty. On both sides of the divide, whether the death is by lynching or by execution, similar emotions are aroused. Outside the prison, crowds gather to cheer when the hearse leaves Georgia's home for its electric chair signalling that a death has occurred. Those cheers are not unlike those of the hordes who took excursion trains to witness lynchings. Meanwhile, the burden of sadness descends on the home community of the man killed.

That burden teaches little to the frustrated, unemployed young men other than to be defiant. If they turn to crime, the possibility of the death penalty does not deter them. And those in power learn nothing from that fact. Instead, they call for the carrying out of more death sentences. . . .

Poor and Black in America

Rather than being held in slavery as most of the black poor were in 1857, the present-day equal opportunity poor are being made criminals. As one observer has said, we are creating a nation of felons, who will, if released, have no means of re-entry into the society of the employed. Instead of considering that future, programs of rehabilitation are scrapped in favor of retributive punishment. The response of many in the majority to an undernourished portion of their own society is not analysis, but slogans like, "tough on crime," "three strikes, you're out," and condemnation of "welfare cheats."

And the ultimate expression of this contempt for the useless and, therefore, encouraged to be the dangerous, is the imposition of the death penalty. The steps to attempt to rescue those sentenced to death are termed "frivolous appeals." The rich are not executed; it is the poor and, because race does still play a part, disproportionately, the black.

Finally, to return to the question of societal uses of violence, there is, despite the connections suggested, one crucial difference between both the merciless disciplining of slaves and the lynchings of their descendants on one hand and, on the other, those formally executed. Those earlier cruelties were outside the law; with the death penalty, it is the state—which is to say, we the people—who are the killers.

The Death Penalty
Is Fair

WALTER BERNS AND JOSEPH BESSETTE

The end of the twentieth century saw a heightened interest in issues related to the death penalty. The high-profile cases of Oklahoma City bombing conspirator Terry Nichols and mail bomber Theodore Kaczynski drew the public into the debate over when a death sentence is fair and appropriate. In the Wall Street Journal *piece that follows, Walter Berns and Joseph Bessette examine the issue of fairness and capital punishment since* Furman v. Georgia, *the 1972 case in which the U.S. Supreme Court ruled that the death penalty statutes at the time violated the Eighth Amendment's prohibition against cruel and unusual punishment because the penalty was being arbitrarily applied. Berns and Bessette conclude that the post-Furman Supreme Court rulings have limited the imposition of the death penalty to only the most heinous cases and that therefore it is no longer arbitrary or cruel. Walter Berns is a resident scholar at the American Enterprise Institute in Washington, D.C. He is the author of* Making Patriots *and the editor of* After the People Vote: A Guide to the Electoral College. *Joseph Bessette is a professor of government and ethics at Claremont College in California. He is the author of* The Mild Voice of Reason: Deliberating Democracy and American National Government.

T he death penalty is much in the news. With jurors failing to agree on a sentence for Oklahoma City bombing conspirator Terry Nichols, he will escape the maximum legal punishment for his part in the deaths of eight federal agents (though an Oklahoma jury may eventually sentence him to die if he is convicted of murdering the 160 other victims). Meanwhile, Theodore Kaczynski's Unabomber prosecution continues its halting pace toward what all must now assume will be his execution—after, of course, excruciating delays while the case is appealed to various courts. The U.S. Supreme Court has already refused the last challenged to the execution of spree killer Karla Faye Tucker, who on Feb. 3 [1998] will become the first woman to receive Texas's lethal injection—unless, that is, Gov. George W. Bush decides not to sign her death warrant.

Gov. Bush faces an enormously weighty decision, and so may take some comfort in the knowledge that signing a death warrant was a problem, too, for Abraham Lincoln. "You do not know how hard it is to let a human being die," he said, "when you feel that a stroke of your pen will save him."

Lincoln's misgivings had nothing whatever to do with the legality of capital punishment; as he read it, the Constitution gave him the power to authorize a death sentence when it gave him the power to "grant reprieves." The opponents of capital punishment would applaud his all-too-human misgivings, but deplore his constitutional judgment—which, as it turned out, is today shared by the Supreme Court.

Post-*Furman v. Georgia* Era

True, the court's 1972 decision in *Furman v. Georgia* held that, when imposed in an arbitrary or capricious manner, the death penalty violated the Eighth Amendment's prohibition of "cruel and unusual punishments." Because, under the state laws then in force, only an unfortunate few of those convicted of a capital crime were being sentenced to death, Justice Potter Stewart likened it to "being struck by lightning." The Constitution, he said, could not permit "this unique penalty to be so wantonly and so freakishly imposed."

But this did not put an end to capital punishment. Within a few years, 35 states rewrote their death-penalty statutes, and in 1976, in cases from Georgia, Texas and Florida, the Supreme Court upheld their constitutionality.

By narrowing the categories of murder for which the death penalty might be imposed, and by requiring separate sentencing hearings during which juries or judges would weigh evidence of aggravating or mitigating circumstances, the new laws ensured, again in Justice Stewart's words, that "sentences of death will not be 'wantonly' or 'freakishly' imposed."

But the issue of arbitrariness has not died. In 1986, Jack Greenberg, writing in the Harvard Law Review, complained that capital punishment continued to be imposed in an "infrequent, random, and erratic fashion." More recently, Hugo Adam Bedau, perhaps the nation's leading academic opponent of capital punishment, denied that the new laws succeeded in "winnowing the worst from the (merely) bad" offenders. The few actually sentenced to death—5,533 since 1976, of whom 403 have in fact been executed—are, he said, simply "the losers in an arbitrary lottery."

The opponents have now gained support from an unlikely quarter. Writing in these pages last month [December 1997]. Princeton Prof. John J. Dilulio repeated the lottery analogy, asserting that the administration of the death penalty in the U.S. is, and is likely to remain, "arbitrary and capricious," and thus ought to be abolished. Because he is known otherwise to be a proponent of harsh punishment, Mr. Dilulio's judgment ought to carry weight. On this subject, however, he is surely mistaken.

No Longer Arbitrary or Cruel

Rather than being arbitrary and capricious, the system now in place serves as a filter, reserving the death penalty for the worst offenders. This is demonstrably the case in

Illinois. In August 1996, state prosecutors compiled a list of the 174 persons then on death row in Illinois, with a description of the murder (or murders) committed by each offender. A comparison of this information with the data on homicides collected by the FBI and the Justice Department's Bureau of Justice Statistics reveals the dramatic difference between the crimes committed by the offenders on death row in Illinois and other murderers:

- 20% of those on the Illinois death row committed murders during the commission of a rape or sexual assault, compared with well under 1% of all murderers;
- 10% of the condemned committed murders during a burglary or home invasion, compared with less than 1% of all murders;
- 13% of the condemned had murdered a child, compared with 4% of all murders;
- 37% of the condemned committed murders involving more than one victim, compared with 4% of all murders.

These statistics do not succeed in conveying the truly despicable nature of the crimes committed by those on death row in Illinois. The first offender in this (alphabetically ordered) list murdered two Chicago police officers; the second murdered a Chicago police officer by running him down with an automobile; the third beat to death an 86-year-old woman with her walking cane; the fourth shot and killed four persons during a drug-related robbery; the fifth murdered his girlfriend's 16-month-old daughter by denying her food and exposing her to subfreezing temperatures; the sixth shot to death an 86-year-old man during a robbery; the seventh, while dressed as a priest, committed a murder-for-hire of an 81-year-old widow by shooting her twice in the back of the head; the eighth, during an armed robbery, shot and killed one man and wounded another; the ninth raped and murdered a 34-year-old woman as she walked to catch a bus; and the 10th shot and killed three men in a dispute over money.

There are no barroom brawls here, no domestic disputes

that got out of hand, no "heat of passion" crimes that are so common among homicides in the U.S. These are brutal, cold-blooded murders, often involving other felonies, and often committed against the most vulnerable of victims. An examination of the lists of those on death row in the other 37 capital-punishment states would probably show that they, too, reserve the death penalty for the worst offenders.

Indeed, it could hardly be otherwise. In the post-*Furman* era, and at the insistence of the Supreme Court, the death-penalty states have carved out from first-degree murder (already a subset of all homicides) a still narrower category of the most heinous killings and have rendered them alone subject to capital punishment. This system, which imposes the death penalty on a few hundred of the 12,000 persons convicted each year of homicide, cannot be described as arbitrary or capricious.

Nor can it be described as cruel. During his four years as president, and despite his misgivings, Lincoln authorized the executions of 267 soldiers and sailors, men sentenced to death for desertion or for sleeping on watch, but none of them so deserving of death as the men on the Illinois list—to say nothing of mass murderer John Gacey; Richard Allen Davis, the killer of 12-year-old Polly Klaas; or, to bring this up to date, the notorious Timothy McVeigh.

Women Are No Longer Spared the Death Penalty Because of Their Gender

ELIZABETH RAPAPORT

In the excerpt that follows, Elizabeth Rapaport discusses the executions of four women that have taken place since the 1972 Supreme Court ruling in Furman v. Georgia, *which found that the death penalty statutes in effect at the time violated the Eighth Amendment's prohibition against cruel and unusual punishment. Since that ruling, judges and juries have been obliged to base their decisions to impose the death penalty on the heinousness of the crime, whether committed by a man or a woman. Rapaport considers the level of willingness exhibited by judges and governors to execute these convicted female murderers as well as the extent of public outcry that accompanies their death sentences and executions. She concludes that in the near future, the execution of women will not provoke any special moral outrage. Elizabeth Rapaport is a professor at the University of New Mexico School of Law. She also serves on the New Mexico state bar's Task Force to Consider the Administration of the Death Penalty.*

Elizabeth Rapaport, "Equality of the Damned: The Execution of Women on the Cusp of the 21st Century," *Ohio Northern University Law Review*, vol. XXVI, 2000, pp. 588–600.

Throughout American history, from early colonial times until the pre-*Furman* [*v. Georgia*, U.S. Supreme Court case in which the death penalty was ruled unconstitutional] moratorium period during which no executions took place, women have been executed; females account for approximately 3% of all executions, or 556 women, from 1632 until the execution of Elizabeth Duncan in California in 1962. In the period from 1930, when the federal government began collecting information about capital punishment until, 1962, the Bureau of Justice Statistics tallies thirty-two executions, or one a year. We have always executed women. Yet, before *Furman*, it was normal, as a matter of both law and culture, to treat gender as relevant to the assessment of guilt and punishment. Thus, it was unremarkable for Governor West of Oregon to explain his grant of clemency to a female death row prisoner in 1908 in the following terms: "'When I saw that woman in the penitentiary (the only one there), it made me sick, and so I turned her loose.'"

A more remarkable example of chivalry was the 1941 petition from thirty San Quentin inmates to the Governor of California opposing the execution of Eithel Spinelli; her execution, they claimed, would be dishonorable, a blot on the reputation of the state and "repulsive to the people of California" because of her sex and her status as a mother. The signers offered to draw straws to go to the gas chamber in her stead if clemency was refused. Whether the law was more kind or unkind to women, on balance, under this dispensation, is a matter of controversy that will not concern me here. Beginning in the late 1960's, it became a violation of equal protection to favor or disfavor either sex in sentencing schemes or their application. When the moratorium period ended and the capital prisoners of the new era began to suffer execution in the late 1970's and early 1980's, all those charged with doing justice in capital cases were obliged to proceed on the basis of the equal susceptibility of men and women to the forfeit of life for murders of extraordinary heinousness.

The Execution of Women in the Post-*Furman* Era

Four women have been executed since the resumption of executions after the moratorium; the first man was executed in 1977, the first woman, Velma Barfield, in 1984. She was the second person to be executed in North Carolina after the moratorium, and the twenty-ninth person to be executed in the country. The year of her execution witnessed a substantial rise in the number of people executed annually, twenty-one; there had been a total of eleven executions 1977–83. Thus, one woman was executed early in the history of the modern death penalty era. Her execution, in retrospect, revealed the future of executing women in the era of formal equality. However, both the post-moratorium institution of capital punishment and gender equality were so new in 1984, that it would take another fourteen years and the execution of Karla Faye Tucker [in 1998] before the lessons could be assimilated. In 1984, a Southern governor from an execution state was forced to try to determine the social and political meaning of executing a woman in the first years of the formal egalitarian era. In 1998, another Southern governor from the nation's leading execution state, Texas, had the same political riddle thrust upon him. Before turning to the politics of executing women, let us review the four executions in the post-*Furman* era.

The four executions have all occurred in active execution states, Texas and Florida being respectively the leading and the third-ranked death penalty states. More than two-thirds of all executions that have occurred since the resumption of executions in 1977 have occurred in six states. Texas, the site of two of these executions, accounts for a full third of all executions. The execution of Betty Lou Beets was the 121st of George W. Bush's governorship. Texas, Florida, and North Carolina have consistently ranked among the leading states in numbers of female death row inmates.

Velma Barfield was sentenced to die for the arsenic poisoning of her fiancé. She admitted to poisoning three other people, her mother and an elderly couple who employed Barfield to care for them. She was, additionally, a suspect in the poisoning death of her husband. She claimed she killed in an uncomprehending haze induced by drug addiction, and that she actually killed to cover up thefts carried out to buy prescription tranquilizers. At the time of her execution, she was drug-free, a born-again Christian, and loved by all who knew her, inmates and staff, at the Women's Prison in Raleigh [North Carolina]. The campaign for her clemency was led by Ruth Graham, the wife of evangelist Billy Graham. She was fifty-two and a grandmother when she left this world by way of lethal injection.

Karla Faye Tucker, a drug-addicted prostitute, committed two pickaxe murders in the company of a boyfriend. No one has ever suggested that she was anything but an equal and willing participant in the crimes. She embraced the role of a bad girl in life and in her trial testimony. The murders were almost pointless; the victims happened to be unexpectedly home and asleep when Tucker and her boyfriend arrived to steal some motorcycle parts. There was a history of bad feeling between the killers and the male murder victim. Tucker, who became the sweetheart of death row, and who, while in prison, contracted a white marriage with the prison chaplain, bragged at the time of the killing that she was sexually gratified with every stroke of the pickaxe. In prison, Tucker sobered up and became a devout evangelical Christian. Fascinating and repellent at her trial, she became a media star in the weeks leading up to her execution. Her wan, pixie-ish good looks, her youthfulness, her wry, self-deprecating humor, and her self-possession, articulateness and thoughtfulness, captivated television audiences. She was thirty-eight years old at her death.

Judias Buenoano, born in Panama, was capitally sentenced in 1985, for the poisoning death of her husband. There was evidence that she had poisoned another man successfully and poisoned but failed to kill a third, in each case in order to collect life insurance. She had previously been convicted of drowning her paralyzed son by pushing him out of a canoe. Buenoano underwent no religious or other transformation in prison, never showed remorse, and was supported at the end by no following of her own, other than those who oppose capital punishment generally. She was well liked, accommodating, and now missed among those who knew her while in prison. She was mourned by her daughter, who had hoped for commutation. Judi Buenoano was a fifty-four-year-old grandmother at her death.

Betty Lou Beets was sentenced to die in 1985 for the shooting death of her fifth husband for pecuniary gain, life insurance policies and pension benefits. The police found his body buried in her front yard. They also discovered the body of her fourth husband who had also been shot in the head. Years earlier she had been convicted of shooting and wounding her second husband. Long after her trial, she claimed that she had suffered years of domestic abuse. Her cause was taken up by opponents of domestic abuse. Unlike her Texas death row sister, Karla Faye Tucker, who conducted much of her own campaign for clemency through media interviews, Beets went silent to her death. She was sixty-two years old.

The Execution of Velma Barfield

In 1984, Governor Jim Hunt of North Carolina sought to replace incumbent U.S. Senator Jesse Helms in a close and bitterly contested election. In August of that year a superior court judge, offering no explanation, scheduled the execution of Velma Barfield to occur just days before the election. The execution could have been scheduled as late as November 22. The judge's decision put Governor Hunt in an unenviable position. He was a declared proponent of capital punishment in a state where the death penalty was believed to be favored by 70% of the electorate. But he was identified with the progressive wing of the state's Democratic Party. His advisors feared that the execution of a woman the weekend before the election would keep core liberal supporters, thought to represent his potential margin of victory, at home. Little as the Hunt camp wanted to alienate liberals, blocking the execution could be expected to anger pro–capital punishment voters. Although the Barfield execution was never an explicit election issue, Hunt was struggling to fend off accusations by Helms that he was a weak and vacillating leader who did "'flip-flops' on issues." Complicating matters further, Barfield had won the support of some evangelicals who believed her faith and repentance were sincere. Ruth Graham, wife of evangelist Billy Graham, was the spokeswoman for evangelicals pressing Governor Hunt to commute Barfield's sentence.

Hunt chose the more prudent of two unpalatable choices in late September:

> I cannot in good conscience justify making an exception to the law as enacted by our State Legislature, or overruling those twelve jurors who, after hearing the evidence, concluded that Mrs. Barfield should pay the maximum penalty for her brutal actions.

The risks of losing liberal opponents of the death penalty and alienating religious opposition to the death of a Christian woman had to be embraced. He could not make an exception for a woman in a glaringly visible death penalty case on the eve of the election. More than 77% of the letters the governor's office received from constituents urged Hunt to deny clemency. Whatever chivalry and compassion stirred in the breasts of Jim Hunt and the voters of North Carolina for the fifty-two-year-old grandmother was quelled by the compelling logic of equal justice. Jim Hunt, a New South governor in the late twentieth century, could not grant clemency to Barfield because she was a woman unless he was willing to pay the political price.

In the fall of 1997 Governor George W. Bush was alerted that an execution date would be scheduled for Karla Faye

Tucker after the first of the year. Tucker and Bush would become the protagonists in the highest profile death case that Texas and the United States had seen during his term as governor. Bush as governor had allowed dozens of executions to go forward; he had never granted or by any account seriously considered granting clemency. Unlike Governor Jim Hunt of North Carolina, his support for the death penalty could not be doubted. Bush was on record, and indeed was eager to reassert, that there were two questions he examined in each death case; if the answers were affirmative, he felt bound to allow an execution to proceed:

> Early in my administration, I decided the standards by which I would decide whether to allow an execution to proceed. In every case, I would ask: Is there any doubt about this individual's guilt or innocence? And, have the courts had ample opportunity to review all the legal issues in this case?

Tucker herself unreservedly acknowledged her guilt; she based her petition for clemency not on any alleged judicial errors or procedural defects in her case but on her commitment to Christianity, including opposition to capital punishment. The decision to allow the execution was straightforward in light of Bush's standards, yet he describes the Tucker execution as one of the most difficult passages in his governorship. The reasons are not far to seek and are rather candidly discussed in his campaign biography. Bush quotes from "a front-page story by Texas-based reporter Sam Howe Verhovek [of the *New York Times*]" to convey "the discomfort":

> AS WOMAN'S EXECUTION NEARS, TEXAS SQUIRMS. Texas had put thirty-seven men to death the previous year, the article said, the most executions in a single year in any state in the modern era of capital punishment. "But even for a state with the nation's busiest execution chamber, the looming lethal injection of prisoner No. 777 at the Mountain View Unit here is a milestone," the article continued. "As the execution date nears, an unlikely ar-

ray of sympathizers ranging from Christian conservatives to a juror in her trial are lobbying to save her life in a case that offers a stark political quandary for Mr. Bush and an equally stark picture of society's reluctance—even in a law-and-order state—to execute women."

Bush was to seek re-election as Governor of Texas in 1998 and enter the race for President of the United States in the 2000 election. His political standing as a governor was high, and his prospects in 2000 looked bright. He was more than content to campaign on a record as the governor who far and away led the nation in the number of executions over which he had presided. But the Tucker execution appeared to Bush to present the same hazards that the Barfield execution posed to Jim Hunt in 1984. He feared being punished politically, in Texas and later nationally, by public reaction to the execution of a woman—a young, attractive, white, Christian woman. Tucker's sincerity as a Christian was attested to by none other than Pat Robertson, televangelist and leader of the Christian Coalition, who asked Bush to grant clemency. Governor Bush, who calls himself a "compassionate conservative" and insists upon the depth of importance of Christianity in his own life, had the added burden of maintaining the luster of these attributes while adhering to the law-and-order standards upon which he had staked his political career.

Events as they unfolded taught the same lesson that the Barfield execution had taught in 1984: let us assume that political expedience, not personal conviction, guided Governor Bush's actions from the time he learned of the impending execution date until the death of Karla Faye Tucker in February of 1998. Bush's problem, unvarnished, was that given the belief in public reluctance to execute a woman and a public riveted on a spectacle that had everything—sex, death, and the fate of princes—he was presented with a choice between appearing to bow under pressure and appearing "bloodthirsty." The pressures he describes may well have been more intense than any others in his tenure in office, and the twenty minutes between the insertion of the needle bearing lethal poison into Karla Faye Tucker and the pronouncement of her death may well have been "the longest twenty minutes" of his service in office. But Bush has not been punished for executing "the sweetheart of death row." The reluctance of the public to see women executed was apparently exaggerated or misunderstood. The political backlash never materialized. Two more executions of women have gone forward since Tucker's death, that of Judi Buenoano in Florida, within a few weeks of Tucker's death, and that of Betty Lou Beets in Texas. They attracted relatively scant public interest. Governor Lawton Chiles in Florida and Governor Bush in Texas were released by the Tucker execution from the strain of performing the bowing-to-pressure versus appearing-bloodthirsty calculus. The execution of Buenoano and Beets did not raise the specter of a wroth public taking political reprisals upon a governor who failed to honor their double standard for death. . . .

The Future of Execution of Women in the United States

The near-term future of execution of women in the United States is likely to resemble the recent past. The executions of Judi Buenoano in 1998, and Betty Lou Beets in 2000, were accompanied by only faint echoes of the excitement that swirled around the Barfield and Tucker executions. Unless renewal of abolitionist sentiment forestalls the dramatic increase in the pace of executions of the last few years, we are likely to see further executions of women occur with as little strain as was felt in Buenoano's or Beets' departures. Indeed, with the Beets and Buenoano executions, we have seen a reassertion of the gender stereotyping that has historically dehumanized despised female murderers. Both these women were styled "Black Widows," a label that imposes psychic distance and deploys sexualized fear and hostility. A fifth woman was executed in

Arkansas on May 2, 2000, with similarly modest publicity and no press speculation about whether the Governor would allow the execution of a woman. Whether there will be any lasting repercussions of Karla Faye Tucker's witness for the damned remains to be seen. If so, it will be as part of a renewed movement for abolition for the thousands on death row of both sexes.

The Death Penalty Is Unfair and Should Be Abolished

AUSTIN SARAT

While the death penalty abolitionist movement has roots in early American history, the moratorium movement is a recent development that began in the last decade of the twentieth century. This movement seeks to put executions "on hold" while certain legal and moral concerns are addressed by the states and the courts. In this selection, Austin Sarat analyzes the American Bar Association's 1997 resolution calling for a moratorium on executions. Sarat applauds that resolution, calling it part of the "new abolitionism." Sarat concludes that the moratorium movement, while not a total abolition of the death penalty, is an important step that could ultimately lead to the end of capital punishment in the United States. Austin Sarat is a professor of political science and law at Amherst College. He is the author of When the State Kills: Capital Punishment and the American Condition *and the editor of* Cultural Analysis, Cultural Studies, and the Law: Moving Beyond Legal Realism.

T he new abolitionism was also articulated in a resolution calling for a moratorium [a movement whose aim is to seek to end the death penalty] on state killing passed in February 1997 by the American Bar Association (ABA).

Austin Sarat, *When the State Kills: Capital Punishment and the American Condition*. Princeton, NJ: Princeton University Press, 2001. Copyright © 2001 by Princeton University Press. Reproduced by permission.

Taking us back to *Furman*'s[1] condemnation of the death penalty as "then administered," the ABA resolution proclaimed that the death penalty as "currently administered" is not compatible with central values of our Constitution. Since *Furman* the effort to produce a constitutionally acceptable death penalty has, in the view of the ABA, been to no avail. Thus the ABA "calls upon each jurisdiction that imposes capital punishment not to carry out the death penalty until the jurisdiction implements policies and procedures . . . intended to (1) ensure that death penalty cases are administered fairly and impartially, in accordance with due process, and (2) minimize the risk that innocent people may be executed."

However, the language of the ABA resolution, seems conditional and contingent in its condemnation of death as a punishment. Even as it calls for a cessation of executions it appears to hold out hope for a process of reform in which the death penalty can be brought within constitutionally acceptable norms. As if to leave little doubt of its intention, the ABA resolution concludes by stating that the association "takes no position on the death penalty."

Some might argue that the ABA recommendations, qualified as they seem to be, remain deeply invested in a sentimental narrative—that all we need to do is to stop victimizing those convicted criminals with poor counsel, the erosion of postconviction protections, and racism in order to purify state killing. However, the ABA resolution, despite its explicit refusal to take a position on the ultimate question of the constitutionality of capital punishment, amounts to a call for the abolition, not merely the cessation, of capital punishment. . . . If one takes seriously the conclusions of the report accompanying the ABA's recommendation, then the largest association of lawyers in the country is asking us to save further damage to America by ending the death penalty. In so

1. *Furman v. Georgia* was a 1976 U.S. Supreme Court case whose outcome declared the death penalty as it existed then to be cruel and unusual punishment.

doing the ABA provides a striking response to the continuing anxiety that attends the embrace of the state's ultimate violence. Just as rushing a fresh contingent of troops into a battle going badly may reinvigorate those grown weary in battle even if ultimately it does not stem the tide, so too the ABA's action provides an important vehicle for thinking about capital punishment and the American condition.

The Reasons for a Moratorium

The ABA report provides three reasons for a moratorium on executions, each a crucial component of the new abolitionism. First is the failure of most states to guarantee competent counsel in capital cases. Because most states have no regular public defender systems, they are frequently assigned to indigent capital defendant lawyers with no interest, or experience, in capital litigation. The result often is incompetent defense lawyering, lawyering that has become all the more damaging in light of new rules requiring that defenses cannot be raised on appeal or in habeas proceedings [appeal to federal court] if they are not raised, or if they are waived, at trial. The ABA itself calls for the appointment of "two experienced attorneys at each stage of a capital case." While, in theory, individual states could provide competent counsel in death cases, and while there is ample evidence to suggest the value of skilled lawyers in preventing the imposition of death sentences, the political climate in the United States as it touches on the crime problem suggests that there is, in fact, little prospect for a widespread embrace of the ABA's call for competent counsel.

The second basis for the ABA's recommended moratorium is the recent erosion in postconviction protections for capital defendants. While the ABA notes that "the federal courts should consider claims that were not properly raised in state court if the reason for the default was counsel's ignorance or neglect and that a prisoner should be permitted to file a second or successive federal petition if it raises a new claim that undermines confidence in his or her guilt or the appropriateness of the death sentence," the direction of legal change is, as I already have noted, in the opposite direction. Today courts in the United States are prepared to accept that some innocent people, or some defendants who do not deserve death, will be executed. As Justice [William] Rehnquist observed in *Herrera v. Collins*, "due process does not require that every conceivable step be taken, at whatever cost, to eliminate the possibility of convicting an innocent person."

For Rehnquist, what is true in the general run of criminal cases is also true in death cases. If a few errors are made, a few innocent lives taken, that is simply the price of a system that is able to execute anyone at all. In Rehnquist's view finality in capital cases is more important than an extended, and extremely frustrating, quest for justice. For him, and others like him, the apparent impotence of the state, its inability to turn death sentences into executions, is more threatening to its legitimacy than a few erroneous, undeserved deaths at the hands of the state. Here again what the ABA asks for, namely a restoration of some of the previously available habeas remedies, is theoretically conceivable. Yet like efforts to improve the quality of defense counsel in capital cases, it is hardly a likely or near-term possibility.

The third reason for the ABA's call for a moratorium is the "longstanding patterns of racial discrimination . . . in courts around the country," patterns of discrimination that have repeatedly been called to the attention of the judiciary and cited by anti-death penalty lawyers as reasons why the death penalty violates the Fourteenth Amendment guarantee of equal protection. The ABA report cites research showing that defendants are more likely to receive a death sentence if their victim is white rather than black, and that in some jurisdictions African Americans tend to receive the death penalty more than do white defendants. The report calls for the development of "effective mechanisms" to eliminate racial prejudice in capital cases, yet does not identify what such mechanisms would be. Indeed, it is not clear that there are any such mechanisms.

The pernicious effects of race in capital sentencing are a function of the persistence of racial prejudice throughout the society combined with the wide degree of discretion necessary to afford individualized justice in capital prosecutions and capital trials. Prosecutors with limited resources may be inclined to allocate resources to cases that attract the greatest public attention, which often will mean cases where the victim was white and his or her assailant black. Participants in the legal system—whether white or black—demonize young black males, seeing them as more deserving of death as a punishment because of their perceived danger. These cultural effects are not remediable in the near term, not so long as we live in a killing state. As [former Justice Harry] Blackmun noted in *Callins*, "we may not be capable of devising procedural or substantive rules to prevent the more subtle and often unconscious forms of racism from creeping into the system . . . discrimination and arbitrariness could not be purged from the administration of capital punishment without sacrificing the equally essential component of fairness-individualized sentencing."

New Abolitionism Gains Momentum

Today the new abolitionism promoted by Blackmun and the ABA seems to be gaining a little momentum. While public opinion polls continue to register the support of the overwhelming majority of Americans for capital punishment, the June 12, 2000, issue of *Newsweek* reported that "For the first time in a generation, the death penalty itself is in the dock—on the defensive at home and especially abroad for being too arbitrary and too prone to error." About the same time, the *New York Times* proclaimed the coming of "the new death penalty politics" saying that "heightened public concern over the fallibility of the criminal justice system [has caused] a dramatic shift in the national debate over capital punishment."

Growing evidence of failures in that system revealed by

the increased availability of DNA testing has been particularly consequential in bringing about this new situation. Indeed since 1972, eighty-seven people have been freed from death row because they were proved innocent after their trials and appeals were completed, an error rate of about one innocent person for every 7 persons executed. This has made it possible for politicians seeking to remain in the mainstream to embrace the new abolitionism.

A remarkable moment for the new abolitionism occurred when, on January 31, 2000, Governor George Ryan of Illinois, a longtime supporter of capital punishment, announced plans to block all executions in that state by granting stays before any scheduled lethal injections are administered. His act effectively imposed a moratorium on the death penalty, the first time this had been done in any state. Ryan said that he was convinced that the death penalty system in Illinois was "fraught with errors" and "broken" and that it should be suspended until thoroughly investigated. Subsequently, Governor Ryan stated that until he can be given a "100% guarantee" against mistaken convictions, he would authorize no more executions.

Following Ryan's announcement, the U.S. Department of Justice initiated its own review "to determine whether the federal death penalty system unfairly discriminates against racial minorities." Moreover, legislation has been introduced in Congress to lessen the chance of unfairness and deadly error by making DNA testing available to both state and federal inmates, and by setting national standards to ensure that competent lawyers are appointed for capital defendants. Other legislation would suspend all executions at the federal and state levels while a national blue-ribbon commission reviews the administration of the death penalty.

Growing Effect of the Moratorium Movement

In May 2000 the New Hampshire legislature became the first to vote for repeal of the death penalty in more than two decades. While this legislation was subsequently vetoed by Governor Jeanne Shaheen, much of its support reflected new abolitionist sentiment. Thus one Republican representative, who like Illinois Governor Ryan had been a longtime supporter of capital punishment, explained his vote for repeal by saying, "There are no millionaires on death row. Can you honestly say that you're going to get equal justice under the law when, if you've got the money, you are going to get away with it."

New and unexpected voices—including such prominent conservatives as the Reverend Pat Robertson and newspaper columnist George Will—have spoken out against what they see as inequality and racial discrimination in the administration of state killing and in favor of a moratorium. A National Committee to Prevent Wrongful Executions, whose members include death penalty supporters such as William S. Sessions, former Texas judge and FBI director in the Reagan and Bush administrations, has called for a reexamination of the process that leads to wrongful death sentences. If all this were not enough to signal the growing significance of the new abolitionism as a force in American politics, George W. Bush in June 2000 used his power as Texas governor to grant his first stay of execution after more than five years in office and after more than 130 people had been executed during his tenure. He did so in order to allow for DNA testing of evidence that linked a condemned man, Ricky McGinn, to the rape of his alleged victim. The news media were quick to note the symbolic significance of this gesture by contrasting it with one provided by Arkansas Governor Bill Clinton when, in January 1992, he interrupted his presidential campaign to return home to preside over the execution of Ricky Ray Rector, a mentally impaired black man convicted of killing a police officer.

Despite these encouraging developments the new abolitionism is still a long way from bringing an end to capital punishment. Yet what its supporters have succeeded in doing is calling our attention to the condition of America, its laws, its culture, its commitments as a way of framing the debate about state killing. They remind us that the post-*Furman* effort to rationalize death sentences has utterly failed and has been replaced by a policy that favors execution while trimming away procedural protection for capital defendants. This situation only exacerbates the incompatibility of state killing and legality. As U.S. Senator Russ Feingold of Wisconsin noted, "At the end of 1999, as we enter a new millennium, our society is still far from fully just. The continued use of the death penalty demeans us. The death penalty is at odds with our best traditions. . . . And it's not just a matter of morality . . . the continued viability of our justice system as a truly just system requires that we do so." For Senator Feingold, as for Justice Blackmun, the ABA, Governor Ryan, and others, the rejection of the death penalty takes the form of an effort to prevent the erosion of the boundaries between state violence and its extralegal counterpart.

Moratorium and the Spirit of *Furman*

This effort, while speaking to some of the most pressing issues facing today's capital punishment system, also captures the spirit of *Furman*. It calls us back to *Furman*'s critique of the practices of capital punishment, to its doubts about whether those practices could be squared with the law's requirements. Yet it radicalizes *Furman* by reminding all Americans of this country's continuing inability, now almost thirty years later, to get state killing right. It reminds us of the spirit of vengeance and cultural division that attends the death penalty and calls on us to embrace the new abolitionism in the spirit of addressing our most pressing social problems so that our future might be better than our past. It offers us the chance to escape the compulsion to think only about victimization, to cast problems of crime and punishment in morally simplistic terms, and to reconsider what this society wishes to be.

In the end, the new abolitionism calls on America to stop

one line of killing that we have within our power to stop, namely capital punishment. It asks us to do so to preserve what we value in our legal institutions. It asks us to do so in order that we might begin the work of healing the divisions in our culture. It asks us to do so in the hope that our present embrace of the killing state is the result of fear rather than venality, misunderstanding rather than clear-headed commitment.

DNA Technology Can Assure the Fairness of the Death Penalty

NEW YORK POST

DNA—deoxyribonucleic acid—evidence was first introduced in American courts in 1986 and is now admitted in all U.S. courts. The following editorial acknowledges the spate of cases in which people convicted of murder have been released from their death sentences by DNA evidence that proves their innocence. However, the editorial concludes that these cases do not show that the death penalty is inherently unjust. Instead, the use of DNA evidence can now prove that the convicted defendant is indeed the actual murderer, thus ensuring the fairness of the death penalty.

Today [June 19, 2001], the U.S. government will enact the ultimate criminal punishment for the second time in as many weeks, following an unprecedented 38-year pause in executions at the federal level. At the same time, arguments in opposition to the death penalty are receiving a receptive hearing in a way they haven't since the early 1970s.

Elite opinion has always leaned against capital punishment, of course. But recently public opinion has taken something of a turn as well. For more than two decades, Americans approved the use of the death penalty by a three-to-one margin. Lately, that has shrunk to two-to-one—still overwhelming, to be sure, but a significant drop in support nonetheless.

This turn has delighted and emboldened death penalty opponents, who believe American public opinion may be evolving to a higher state of consciousness. And it has caused supporters of the death penalty to speculate that the historic crime drop of the 1990s is lulling Americans into a false sense of security.

As Eric Monkkonen argues in his important book, "Murder in New York City," there's a vicious historical cycle to crime and punishment. Periods of slack enforcement lead to jumps in crime. That prompts stricter enforcement and a corresponding drop in crime. As the memory of the crime wave fades, the public becomes disenchanted with the perceived ugliness of strict enforcement. That leads to new slackening. Which leads to new crime. Which leads to new strictness. And so on.

Effects of DNA Technology

That is certainly true, and certainly worrying. But I think there's something more complicated going on here. The shift on capital punishment is almost certainly due to the handful of recent cases in which innocent people have been saved from death row by a new examination of the facts and evidence that led to their convictions in the years before DNA-detection technology would have exculpated them.

Death penalty opponents tend to be moral absolutists who believe its imposition is an act of barbarism no matter the circumstances. They have used the exculpations to make the argument that capital punishment is inherently unjust. It might seem that the public-opinion shift, which supports the notion of a "moratorium" of the sort now in place in Illinois,[1] is testimony to their success at making this case.

1. In January 2000, Illinois governor George Ryan imposed a moratorium on the state's death penalty pending a review of the mistaken findings of guilt in the Illinois capital punishment system.

But opponents should probably hesitate before they take too much heart. For the fact of the matter is that even passionate supporters of the death penalty are horrified by the thought of an innocent being put to death by the state. And the existence of DNA evidence points the way not to a ban on capital punishment but to a new consensus in favor of it that the American public will (I believe) find palatable.

DNA Technology Can Assure Fairness

Why? Simple: State and federal sentencing guidelines can be changed that will make it possible to impose the death penalty only in cases where the physical evidence makes it absolutely certain that the accused is indeed the killer. When the evidence is circumstantial, the death penalty will not be sought.

This is the logical extension of the Illinois moratorium, and represents a political and moral solution that will be palatable to Republicans and Democrats of the Clintonite persuasion (who probably oppose the death penalty in their hearts but know a losing cause when they see one).

With this new standard, opponents of capital punishment will be left having to convince Americans that the penalty itself is always unjust, not that the sentence might be carried out unjustly. That's a more honest basis for discussion because it's what they really think anyway.

THE
HISTORY
OF
ISSUES

CHAPTER 4

Moral Issues

THE
HISTORY
OF
ISSUES

Chapter Preface

A discussion of the death penalty in America invites intense moral scrutiny. People question whether it is ever right for the government to kill and, if so, when. Religious leaders often take strong positions on these questions and frequently disagree with each other. For example, Presbyterian minister Jacob J. Vellenga argues that biblical scripture supports the death penalty. He writes, "Jesus was not advocating doing away with capital punishment but urging his followers to live above the law so that law and punishment could not touch them. To live above the law is not the same as abrogating it."

On the other hand, Rabbi Israel Kazis believes that the Mishnah, a document of Jewish law that is based on the Old Testament, prohibits the enforcement of the death penalty. He concludes that the list of regulations about the death penalty in the Mishnah is so comprehensive that it effectively precludes its imposition. Kazis quotes two rabbis in the Mishnah who say, "If we had been in the Sanhedrin (the highest Jewish tribunal during the Greek and Roman periods), no man would ever have been put to death."

Secular as well as religious thinkers hold strong positions on the morality of the death penalty. In his 1792 essay "On Punishing Murder by Death," Benjamin Rush—one of the signers of the Declaration of Independence and one of the first well-known Americans to oppose the death penalty—elaborates upon his belief that society does not have the right to kill one of its citizens. He hopes that generations to follow will eliminate the practice of state-sponsored killing. In contrast, almost two hundred years later, Ernest van den Haag, a distinguished legal scholar and one of the leading proponents of the death penalty in America, wrote an essay examining how the sanctity of the victim's life supports the use of the death penalty as an appropriate retribution for murder. He states that everyone is "under sentence of death" and that capital punishment only hastens it.

The following viewpoints represent but a sampling of the divergent opinions about the morality of capital punishment. The following chapter further explores the history of the debate over this issue.

The Death Penalty Is Immoral and Should Be Abolished

BENJAMIN RUSH

Benjamin Rush wrote the essay "On Punishing Murder by Death" in 1792 in order to elaborate on his brief comments on the wrongness of capital punishment that were contained in an earlier article. In the following excerpt from his essay, Rush explains his primary point that society has no right to take away the life of any of its citizens. He also takes issue with arguments that the tenets of Christianity support the infliction of death by the governing powers. He fears that the death penalty will not be abolished in his generation. He looks to future generations to eliminate what he considers a cruel practice. Born in 1745, Benjamin Rush was educated in both Scotland and the American colonies. As a physician, Rush researched and promoted many groundbreaking methods of medical treatment. As a political and social scientist, he was one of the signers of the Declaration of Independence. His interest in criminal justice led him to take a stand as one of the first Americans of renown to oppose the death penalty. His essays on the need to abolish capital punishment continue to influence jurists and philosophers in modern times.

In an essay upon the effects of public punishments upon criminals and upon society, published in the second volume of the *American Museum*, I hinted, in a short para-

---

Benjamin Rush, "On Punishing Murder by Death," 1792.

graph, at the injustice of punishing murder by death. I shall attempt in the following essay, to support that opinion, and to answer all the objections that have been urged against it.

I. Every man possesses an absolute power over his own liberty and property, but not over his own life. When he becomes a member of political society, he commits the disposal of his liberty and property to his fellow citizens; but as he has no right to dispose of his life, he cannot commit the power over it to any body of men. To take away life, therefore, for any crime, is a violation of the first political compact.

Death Penalty Is Contrary to Reason and Order

II. The punishment of murder by death, is contrary to reason, and to the order and happiness of society.

1. It lessens the horror of taking away human life, and thereby tends to multiply murders.

2. It produces murder, by its influence upon people who are tired of life, and who, from a supposition, that murder is a less crime than suicide, destroy a life (and often that of a near connexion) and afterwards deliver themselves up to justice, that they may escape from their misery by means of a halter.

3. The punishment of murder by death, multiplies murders, from the difficulty it creates of convicting persons who are guilty of it. Humanity, revolting at the idea of the severity and certainty of a capital punishment, often steps in, and collects such evidence in favour of a murderer, as screens him from justice altogether, or palliates his crime into manslaughter. If the punishment of murder consisted in long confinement, and hard labor, it would be proportioned by the measure of our feelings of justice, and every member of society would be a watchman or a magistrate, to apprehend a destroyer of human life, and to bring him to punishment.

4. The punishment of murder by death, checks the op-

erations of universal justice, by preventing the punishment of every species of murder. Quack doctors—frauds of various kinds—and a licentious press, often destroy life, and sometimes with malice of the most propense nature. If murder were punished by confinement and hard labour, the authors of the numerous murders that have been mentioned, would be dragged forth, and punished according to their deserts. How much order and happiness would arise to society from such a change in human affairs! But who will attempt to define these species of murder, or to prosecute offenders of this stamp, if death is to be the punishment of the crime after it is admitted, and proved to be wilful murder?—only alter the punishment of murder, and these crimes will soon assume their proper names, and probably soon become as rare as murder from common acts of violence. . . .

5. The punishment of murder by death, has been proved to be contrary to the order and happiness of society by the experiments of some of the wisest legislators in Europe. The Empress of Russia, the King of Sweden, and the Duke of Tuscany, have nearly extirpated murder from their dominions, by converting its punishment into the means of benefiting society, and reforming the criminals who perpetrate it.

III. The punishment of murder by death, is contrary to divine revelation. A religion which commands us to forgive and even to do good to our enemies, can never authorise the punishment of murder by death. "Vengeance is mine," said the Lord; "I will repay." It is to no purpose to say here, that this vengeance is taken out of the hands of an individual, and directed against the criminal by the hand of government. It is equally an usurpation of the prerogative of heaven, whether it be inflicted by a single person, or by a whole community.

Here I expect to meet with an appeal from the letter and spirit of the gospel, to the law of Moses [moral requirements of the Old Testament], which declares, that "he that killeth a man shall surely be put to death." Forgive, indulgent heaven! the ignorance and cruelty of man, which by the misapplication of this text of scripture, has so long and so often stained the religion of Jesus Christ with folly and revenge.

The following considerations, I hope, will prove that no argument can be deduced from this law, to justify the punishment of murder by death. On the contrary, that several arguments against it, may be derived from a just and rational explanation of that part of the levitical institutions.

1. There are many things in scripture *above*, but nothing *contrary* to reason. Now, the punishment of murder by death, is *contrary* to reason. It cannot, therefore, be agreeable to the will of God.

2. The order and happiness of society cannot fail of being agreeable to the will of God. But the punishment of murder by death, destroys the order and happiness of society. It must therefore be contrary to the will of God.

3. Many of the laws given by Moses, were accommodated to the ignorance and "hardness of heart" of the ancient Jews. Hence their divine legislator expressly says, "I gave them statutes that were *not good*, and judgments whereby *they should not live.*" Of this, the law which respects divorces, and the law of retaliation, which required "an eye for an eye, and a tooth for a tooth," are remarkable instances.

But we are told, that the punishment of murder by death, is founded not only on the law of Moses, but upon a positive precept given to Noah [warned by God of the flood that would destroy the world] and his posterity, that "whoso sheddeth man's blood, by man shall his blood be shed." In order to show that this text does not militate against my proposition, I shall beg leave to transcribe a passage from an essay on crimes and punishments, published by the Reverend Mr. Turner, in the second volume of the Manchester memoirs. "I hope," says this ingenious author, "that I shall not offend any one, by taking the liberty to put my own sense upon this celebrated passage [from the Bible, Rev. 15:10], and to inquire, why it should be deemed a precept at all. To me, I confess, it appears to contain nothing more than a declaration of what will generally happen; and in this view, to stand exactly upon the same ground with such passages as the following: "He that leadeth into captivity shall go into captivity." "He that taketh up the sword, shall perish by the sword." The form of expression is exactly the same in each of the texts; why, then, may they not all be interpreted in the same manner, and considered, not as commands, but as denunciations, and if so, the magistrate will be no more bound by the text in Genesis, to punish murder with death, than he will by the text in the Revelations, to sell every Guinea captain to our West India planters; and yet, however just and proper such a proceeding might be, I suppose no one will assert that the magistrate is bound to it by that, or any other text in the scriptures, or that that alone would be admitted as a sufficient reason for so extraordinary a measure."

If this explanation of the precept given to Noah, be not satisfactory, I shall mention another. Soon after the flood, the infancy and weakness of society rendered it impossible to punish murder by *confinement.* There was therefore no medium between inflicting death upon a murderer, and suffering him to escape with impunity, and thereby to perpetrate more acts of violence against his fellow creatures. It pleased God in this condition of the world to permit a *less* in order to prevent a *greater* evil. He therefore commits *for a while* his exclusive power over human life, to his creatures for the safety and preservation of an infant society, which might otherwise have perished, and with it, the only stock of the human race. The command indirectly implies that the crime of murder was not punished by death in the mature state of society which existed before the flood. Nor is this the only instance upon record in the scriptures in which God has delegated his power over human life to his creatures. Abraham expresses no surprise at the command which God gave him to sacrifice his son. He submits to it as a precept founded in reason and natural justice, for nothing could be more obvious than that the giver of life had a right to claim it *when* and in *such manner* as he pleased. 'Till men are able to give life, it becomes them to tremble at the thought of *taking it* away. Will a man rob God?—Yes—he robs him of what is infinitely dear to him—of his darling attribute of *mercy*, every time he deprives a fellow creature of life.

4. If the Mosaic law with respect to murder, be obligatory upon Christians, it follows that it is equally obligatory upon them to punish adultery, blasphemy, and other capital crimes that are mentioned in the levitical law, by death. Nor is this all: it justifies the extirpation of the Indians, and the enslaving of the Africans; for the command to the Jews to destroy the Canaanites, and to make slaves of their heathen neighbours, is as positive as the command which declares, "that he that killeth a man, shall surely be put to death."

5. Every part of the levitical law, is full of types of the Messiah. May not the punishment of death, inflicted by it, be intended to represent the demerit and consequences of sin, as the cities of refuge were the offices of the Messiah?

6. The imperfection and severity of these laws were probably intended farther—to illustrate the perfection and mildness of the gospel dispensation. It is in this manner that God has manifested himself in many of his acts. He created darkness first, to illustrate by comparison the beauty of light; and he permits sin, misery, and death in the moral world, that he may hereafter display more illustriously the transcendent glories of righteousness, happiness, and immortal life. This opinion is favoured by St. Paul, who says, "the law made nothing perfect," and that "it was a shadow of good things to come."

How delightful to discover such an exact harmony between the dictates of reason, the order and happiness of society, and the precepts of the gospel! There is a perfect unity in truth. Upon all subjects—in all ages—and in all countries—truths of every kind agree with each other.

It has been said, that the common sense of all nations, and particularly of savages, is in favour of punishing murder by death.

The common sense of all nations is in favor of the commerce and slavery of their fellow creatures. But this does not take away from their immorality. Could it be proved that the Indians punish murder by death, it would not establish the right of man over the life of a fellow creature, for revenge we know in its utmost extent is the universal and darling passion of all savage nations. The practice moreover, (if it exist) must have originated in *necessity;* for a people who have no settled place of residence, and who are averse from all labour, could restrain murder in no other way. But I am disposed to doubt whether the Indians punish murder by death among their own tribes. In all those cases where a life is taken away by an Indian of a *foreign* tribe, they always demand the satisfaction of *life* for *life*. But this practice is founded on a desire of preserving a balance in their numbers and power; for among nations which consist of only a few warriors, the loss of an individual often destroys this balance, and thereby exposes them to war or extermination. It is for the same purpose of keeping up an equality in numbers and power, that they often adopt captive children into their nations and families. What makes this explanation of the practice of punishing murder by death among the Indians more probable, is, that we find the same bloody and vindictive satisfaction is required of a foreign nation, whether the person lost, be killed by an accident, or by premeditated violence. Many facts might be mentioned from travellers to prove that the Indians do not punish murder by death within the jurisdiction of their own tribes. I shall mention only one which is taken from the Rev. Mr. John Megapolensis's account of the Mohawk Indians, lately published in Mr. Hazard's historical collection of state papers.—"There is no punishment, (says our author) here for murder, but every one is his own avenger. The friends of the deceased revenge themselves upon the murderer until peace is made with the next akin. But although they are so cruel, yet there are not half so many murders committed among them as among Christians, notwithstanding their severe laws, and heavy penalties."

It has been said, that the horrors of a guilty conscience proclaim the justice and necessity of death, as a punishment for murder. I draw an argument of another nature from this fact. Are the horrors of conscience the punishment that God inflicts upon murder? why, then, should we shorten or destroy them by death, especially as we are taught to direct the most atrocious murderers to expect pardon in the future world? no, let us not counteract the government of God in the human breast: let the murderer live—but let it be to suffer the reproaches of a guilty conscience: let him live, to make compensation to society for the injury he has done it, by robbing it of a citizen: let him live to maintain the family of the man whom he has murdered: let him live, that the punishment of his crime may become universal: and lastly let him live—that murder may be extirpated from the list of human crimes!

Let us examine the conduct of the moral ruler of the world towards the first murderer: see Cain [first son of Adam and Eve] returning from his field, with his hands reeking with the blood of his brother! Do the heavens gather blackness, and does a flash of lightning blast him to the earth? no. Does his father Adam, the natural legislator and judge of the world, inflict upon him the punishment of death?—No; the infinitely wise God becomes his judge and executioner. He expels him from the society of which he was a member. He fixes in his conscience a never-dying worm. He subjects him to the necessity of labor; and to secure a duration of his punishment, proportioned to his crime, he puts a mark or prohibition upon him, to prevent his being put to death, by weak and angry men; declaring, at the same time, that "whosoever slayeth Cain, vengeance shall be taken on him seven-fold."

Judges, attorneys, witnesses, juries and sheriffs, whose office it is to punish murder by death, I beseech you to pause, and listen to the voice of reason and religion, before you convict or execute another fellow-creature for murder!

But I despair of making such an impression upon the present citizens of the United States, as shall abolish the absurd and un-Christian practice. From the connection of this essay with the valuable documents of the late revolution contained in the American Museum, it will probably descend to posterity. To you, therefore, the unborn generations of the next century, I consecrate this humble tribute to justice. You will enjoy in point of knowledge, the meridian of a day, of which we only perceive the twilight. You will often review with equal contempt and horror, the indolence, ignorance and cruelty of your ancestors. The grossest crimes shall not exclude the perpetrators of them from your pity. You will *fully* comprehend the extent of the discoveries and precepts of the gospel, and you will be actuated, I hope, by its gentle and forgiving spirit. You will see many modern opinions in religion and government turned upside downwards, and many new connexions established between cause and effect. From the importance and destiny of every human soul, you will acquire new ideas of the dignity of human nature, and of the infinite value of every act of benevolence that has for its object, the bodies, the souls, and the lives of your fellow-creatures. You will love the whole human race, for you will perceive that you have a common Father, and you will learn to imitate him by converting those punishments to which their folly or wickedness have exposed them, into the means of their reformation and happiness.

The Death Penalty Is Sanctioned by God

JACOB J. VELLENGA

Believing that the death penalty is sanctioned by God, Jacob J. Vellenga takes issue with those Christians who argue that capital punishment is not supported by biblical scripture or who call it state-sponsored murder. In the next selection he examines both the Old and New Testaments and concludes that the Bible mandates capital punishment for murderers. Vellenga encourages all who believe in the authority of the Bible to search the scriptures, where they will find support for capital punishment laws. Jacob J. Vellenga served on the National Board of Administration of the United Presbyterian Church and as associate executive of the United Presbyterian Church in the United States.

T he Church at large is giving serious thought to capital punishment. Church councils and denominational assemblies are making strong pronouncements against it. We are hearing such arguments as: "Capital punishment brutalizes society by cheapening life." "Capital punishment is morally indefensible." "Capital punishment is no deterrent to murder." "Capital punishment makes it impossible to rehabilitate the criminal."

But many of us are convinced that the Church should not meddle with capital punishment. Church members should be strong in supporting good legislation, militant against wrong laws, opposed to weak and partial law en-

---

Jacob J. Vellenga, "Is Capital Punishment Wrong?" *Christianity Today*, vol. 4, October 12, 1959, pp. 7–9.

forcement. But we should be sure that what we endorse or what we oppose is intimately related to the common good, the benefit of society, the establishment of justice, and the upholding of high moral and ethical standards.

There is a good reason for saying that opposition to capital punishment is not for the common good but sides with evil; shows more regard for the criminal than the victim of the crime; weakens justice and encourages murder; is not based on Scripture but on a vague philosophical system that makes a fetish of the idea that the taking of life is wrong, under every circumstance, and fails to distinguish adequately between killing and murder, between punishment and crime.

Capital punishment is a controversial issue upon which good people are divided, both having high motives in their respective convictions. But capital punishment should not be classified with social evils like segregation, racketeering, liquor traffic, and gambling.

These evils are clearly antisocial, while capital punishment is a matter of jurisprudence established for the common good and benefit of society. Those favoring capital punishment are not to be stigmatized as heartless, vengeful, and lacking in mercy, but are to be respected as advocating that which is the best for society as a whole. When we stand for the common good, we must of necessity be strongly opposed to that behavior which is contrary to the common good.

Capital Punishment and the Old Testament

From time immemorial the conviction of good society has been that life is sacred, and he who violates the sacredness of life through murder must pay the supreme penalty. This ancient belief is well expressed in Scripture: "Only you shall not eat flesh with its life, that is, its blood. For your lifeblood I will surely require a reckoning; of every beast I will require it and of man; of every man's brother I will require the life of man. Whoever sheds the blood of man, by man shall his blood be shed; for God made man in his own image" (Gen. 9:4–6). Life is sacred. He who violates the law must pay the supreme penalty, just because life is sacred. Life is sacred since God made man in His image. There is a distinction here between murder and penalty.

Many who oppose capital punishment make a strong argument out of the Sixth Commandment: "Thou shalt not kill" (Exod. 20:13). But they fail to note the commentary on that Commandment which follows: "Whoever strikes a man so that he dies shall be put to death. . . . If a man willfully attacks another to kill him treacherously, you shall take him from my altar that he may die" (Exod. 21:12,14). It is faulty exegesis to take a verse of Scripture out of its context and interpret it without regard to its qualifying words.

The Exodus reference is not the only one referring to capital punishment. In Leviticus 24:17 we read: "He who kills a man shall be put to death." Numbers 35:30–34 goes into more detail on the subject: "If any one kills a person, the murderer shall be put to death on the evidence of witnesses; but no person shall be put to death on the testimony of one witness. Moreover you shall accept no ransom for the life of a murderer who is guilty of death; but he shall be put to death. . . . You shall not thus pollute the land in which you live; for blood pollutes the land, and no expiation can be made for the land, for the blood that is shed in it, except by the blood of him who shed it. You shall not defile the land in which you live, in the midst of which I dwell; for I the Lord dwell in the midst of the people of Israel." (Compare Deut. 17:6–7 and 19:11–13.)

Deuteronomy 19:4–6,10 distinguishes between accidental killing and wilful murder: "If any one kills his neighbor unintentionally without having been at enmity with him in time past . . . he may flee to one of these cities [cities of refuge] and save his life; lest the avenger of blood in hot anger pursue the manslayer and overtake him, because the way is long, and wound him mortally, though the man did not deserve to die, since he was not at enmity with his neighbor in time past . . . lest innocent blood be shed in your land which the Lord your God gives you for an inheritance, and so the guilt of bloodshed be upon you."

The cry of the prophets against social evils was not only directed against discrimination of the poor, and the oppression of widows and orphans, but primarily against laxness in the administration of justice. They were opposed to the laws being flouted and criminals not being punished. A vivid expression of the prophet's attitude is recorded in Isaiah: "Justice is turned back, and righteousness stands afar off; for truth has fallen in the public squares, and uprightness cannot enter. . . . The Lord saw it and it displeased him that there was no justice. He saw that there was no man, and wondered that there was no one to intervene; then his own arm brought him victory, and his righteousness upheld him. He put on righteousness as a breastplate, and a helmet of salvation upon his head; he put on garments of vengeance for clothing and wrapped himself in a fury as a mantle. According to their deeds, so will he repay, wrath to his adversaries, requital to his enemies" (Isa. 59:14–18).

Capital Punishment and the New Testament

The teachings of the New Testament are in harmony with the Old Testament. Christ came to fulfill the law, not to destroy the basic principles of law and order, righteousness and justice. In Matthew 5:17–20 we read: "Think not that I have come to abolish the law and the prophets; I have come not to abolish them but to fulfill them. For truly, I say to you, till heaven and earth pass away, not an iota, not a dot, will pass from the law until all is accomplished. . . . For I tell you, unless your righteousness exceeds that of the scribes and Pharisees, you will never enter the kingdom of heaven."

Then Christ speaks of hate and murder: "You have heard that it was said to the men of old, 'You shall not kill; and whoever kills shall be liable to judgment [capital punishment].' But I say to you that everyone who is angry with his brother shall be liable to judgment [capital punishment]" (Matt. 5:21–22). It is evident that Jesus was not condemning the established law of capital punishment, but was actually saying that hate deserved capital punishment. Jesus was not advocating doing away with capital punishment but urging his followers to live above the law so that law and punishment could not touch them. To live above the law is not the same as abrogating it.

The Church, the Body of Christ, has enough to do to evangelize and educate society to live above the law and positively to influence society to high and noble living by maintaining a wide margin between right and wrong. The early Christians did not meddle with laws against wrong doing. Paul expresses this attitude in his letter to the Romans: "Therefore, he who resists the authorities resists what God has appointed, and those who resist will incur judgment. For rulers are not a terror to good conduct, but to bad. . . . for he is God's servant for your good. But if you do wrong, be afraid, for he does not bear the sword in vain; he is the servant of God to execute his wrath on the wrongdoer" (13:2–4).

Christianity and Justice

The early Christians suffered many injustices and were victims of inhuman treatment. Many became martyrs because of their faith. Consequently, they were often tempted to take the law in their own hands. But Paul cautioned them: "Beloved, never avenge yourselves, but leave it to the wrath of God; for it is written, 'Vengeance is mine, I will repay, says the Lord.' No, 'if your enemy is hungry, feed him; if he is thirsty, give him drink; for by so doing you will heap burning coals upon his head'" (Rom. 12: 19–21).

There is not a hint of indication in the New Testament that laws should be changed to make it lenient for the wrongdoer. Rather the whole trend is that the Church leave matters of justice and law enforcement to the government in power. "Let every person be subject to the governing authorities. For there is no authority except from God, and those that exist have been instituted by God" (Rom. 13:1). Note the juxtaposition of love to enemies with a healthy respect for government. The Christian fellowship is not to take law in its own hands, for God has government in his economy in order to take care of matters of justice.

Jesus' words on loving one's enemies, turning the other cheek, and walking the second mile were not propaganda to change jurisprudence, but they were meant to establish a new society not merely made up of law-abiding citizens but those who lived a life higher than the law, so that stealing, adultery, and murder would become inoperative, but not annulled. The law of love, also called the law of liberty, was not presented to do away with the natural laws of society, but to inaugurate a new concept of law written on the heart where the mainsprings of action are born. The Church is ever to strive for superior law and order, not to advocate a lower order that makes wrongdoing less culpable.

Capital Punishment and Redemption

Love and mercy have no stability without agreement on basic justice and fair play. Mercy always infers a tacit recognition that justice and rightness are to be expected. Lowering the standards of justice is never to be a substitute for the concept of mercy. The Holy God does not show mercy contrary to his righteousness but in harmony with it. This is why the awful Cross was necessary and a righteous Christ had to hang on it. This is why God's redemption is always conditioned by one's heart attitude. There is no forgiveness for anyone who is unforgiving. "Forgive us our debts, as we forgive our debtors" (Matt. 6:12). There is no mercy for anyone who will not be merciful. "Blessed are the merciful for they shall obtain mercy" (Matt. 5:7). There is striking similarity to these verses in Psalm 18:25–26: "With the loyal thou dost show thyself loyal; with the blameless man thou dost show thyself blameless; with the pure thou dost show thyself pure; and with the crooked thou dost show thyself perverse."

Professor [and Christian philosopher] C.S. Lewis in his recent book *Reflections on the Psalms* deals with the difficult subject of the spirit of hatred which is in some of the Psalms. He points out that these hatreds had a good motivation. "Such hatreds are the kind of thing that cruelty and injustice, by a sort of natural law, produce. . . . Not to perceive it at all—not even to be tempted to resentment—to accept it as the most ordinary thing in the world—argues a terrifying insensibility. Thus the absence of anger, especially that sort of anger which we call indignation, can, in my opinion, be a most alarming symptom. . . . If the Jews cursed more bitterly than the Pagans this was, I think, at least in part because they took right and wrong more seriously."

Vindictiveness is a sin, but only because a sense of justice has gotten out of hand. The check on revenge must be in the careful and exact administering of justice by society's government. This is the clear teaching of Scripture in both the Old and New Testaments. The Church and individual Christians should be active in their witness to the Gospel of love and forgiveness and ever lead people to the high law of love of God and our neighbors as ourselves; but meanwhile wherever and whenever God's love and mercy are rejected, as in crime, natural law and order must prevail, not as extraneous to redemption but as part of the whole scope of God's dealings with man.

The argument that capital punishment rules out the possibility of repentance for crime is unrealistic. If a wanton killer does not repent when the sentence of death is upon him, he certainly will not repent if he has twenty to fifty years of life imprisonment ahead of him.

We, who are supposed to be Christian, make too much of physical life. Jesus said, "And do not fear those who kill the body but cannot kill the soul; rather fear him who can destroy both soul and body in hell" (Matt. 10:28). Laxness in law tends to send both soul and body to hell. It is more than a pious remark when a judge says to the condemned criminal: "And may God have mercy on your soul." The sentence of death on a killer is more redemptive than the tendency to excuse his crime as no worse than grand larceny.

It is significant that when Jesus voluntarily went the way of the Cross he chose the capital punishment of his day as his instrument to save the world. And when he gave redemption to the repentant thief he did not save him from capital punishment but gave him Paradise instead which was far better. We see again that mercy and forgiveness are something different than being excused from wrongdoing.

Capital Punishment Must Stand

No one can deny that the execution of a murderer is a horrible spectacle. But we must not forget that murder is more horrible. The supreme penalty should be exacted only after the guilt is established beyond the shadow of a doubt and only for wanton, willful, premeditated murder. But the law of capital punishment must stand, no matter how often a jury recommends mercy. The law of capital punishment must stand as a silent but powerful witness to the sacredness of God-given life. Words are not enough to show that life is sacred. Active justice must be administered when the sacredness of life is violated.

It is recognized that this article will only impress those who are convinced that the Scriptures of the Old and New Testament are the supreme authority of faith and practice. If one accepts the authority of Scripture, then the issue of capital punishment must be decided on what Scripture actually teaches and not on the popular, naturalistic ideas of sociology and penology that prevail today. One generation's thinking is not enough to comprehend the implications of the age-old problem of murder. We need the best thinking of the ages on how best to deal with crime and punishment. We need the Word of God to guide us.

The Death Penalty Is Forbidden by Jewish Law

ISRAEL J. KAZIS

The Mishnah is a code of Jewish law that makes up part of the Jewish holy book, the Talmud. In the next selection Israel J. Kazis details the provisions of the Mishnah that relate to capital punishment. He shows how they prohibit—or at least inhibit—the enforcement of the death penalty. These provisions include a proscription against circumstantial evidence, the barring of testimony by those related to the victim by blood or marriage, and the requirement for testimony by two eyewitnesses to the crime. The litany of prohibitions and regulations is so exhaustive as to lead Kazis to conclude that it would be difficult, if not impossible, to ever inflict the death penalty. This, according to Kazis, is the very intent of Jewish law: to prevent the imposition of capital punishment. Israel J. Kazis was rabbi of Temple Mishkan Tefila in Newton, Massachusetts.

In order to understand the Jewish attitude toward capital punishment it is not sufficient to consult the Old Testament on this subject. It is necessary also to consult the Mishnah and the Gemara, which represent the codes of Jewish law compiled after the completion of the Bible. This is necessary because Jewish law was not static. It was dynamic and developmental, undergoing modifications through the centuries in terms of the requirements of different periods and places. This legal evolution had to proceed within a given framework; namely, that Biblical law, because it was divinely revealed, could not be abrogated. Consequently the Rabbis had to resort to legal techniques, which, while not abrogating the law technically, nevertheless made it practically unenforceable. The following two examples will illustrate this procedure:

The Prosbul. According to Biblical law all debts were canceled in the Sabbatical or seventh year (Deut. 15:1–3). Hillel, who lived during the first century, B.C.E., saw that this Biblical law worked a hardship on the commercial economy of his time. Those who had money refused to lend it to those who needed money because these loans would be forfeited in the Sabbatical year. Consequently, Hillel introduced an enactment whereby the creditor could turn over the promissory note to the court which in turn would collect the debts from the debtors. While this enactment did not technically abrogate the Biblical law, inasmuch as the creditor himself did not do the collecting of the debt, it did make the Biblical law unenforceable because, by this enactment, debts were not canceled in the seventh year.

The Law of Retaliation. The Bible provides for "an eye for an eye, a tooth for a tooth" (Lev. 24:20), etc. This law of retaliation was interpreted by the Rabbis in terms of monetary compensation for damages, and hence, physical retaliation was unenforceable.

Capital Punishment. The Bible prescribes capital punishment for fifteen different crimes. However, an investigation of the many provisions and restrictions instituted by the Rabbis in the Mishnah and the Gemara in cases involving capital punishment will show that it became virtually impossible to enforce the death penalty.

Restrictions on Capital Cases

Some of these provisions and regulations are:

1. Cases involving capital punishment had to be tried before a court of twenty-three qualified members.

2. Trustworthy testimony had to be presented by two qualified *eye-witnesses*. This requirement was most difficult to meet because the commission of such crimes is not usually attended by so much publicity.

3. Circumstantial evidence was not admitted. The Talmud gives the following example: "I saw a man chasing another into a ruin; I ran after him and saw a sword in his hand dripping with the other's blood and the murdered man in his death agony. I said to him, You villain! Who killed this man? Either I or you. But what can I do? Your life is not delivered into my hand, for the law says, at the mouth of two witnesses shall he that is to die be put to death" (Sanhedrin 37b).

4. The testimony of those related by blood or marriage is not admissible.

5. Men who were presumed to be lacking in compassion were not to be appointed to the court of twenty-three. In this regard the Talmud says: "We do not appoint to a Sanhedrin (court) an old man, a eunuch and a childless man." [Rabbi Judah HaNassi] adds, "One who is hard-hearted" (Sanhedrin 36b).

6. Witnesses were warned not to testify to anything that was based on their own inference, or that they know only second-hand.

7. Witnesses were interrogated separately about the exact time, place, and persons involved in the crime. If any material discrepancy was discovered in their testimony, the accused was acquitted.

8. Witnesses were asked whether they had warned the accused that he was about to commit a crime for which the penalty was death. Such warning was required.

9. The accused was presumed to be innocent until proven guilty, and every reasonable effort was made in the cross-examination to bring out grounds for finding for the accused.

10. In order to prevent witnesses from conspiring to place the guilt on the accused, they were warned that if

they testified falsely they would be liable to the same penalty which the accused would suffer if he were convicted on the basis of their testimony.

The Contrast Between Criminal and Civil Cases

11. The contrast between procedures in civil cases and criminal cases as shown in the following provisions indicates the kind of restrictions that were imposed upon the deliberations of the court in cases involving criminal offenses:

A. In civil cases a majority of one was sufficient to find for the defendant or the plaintiff. In criminal cases a majority of one was sufficient to find for the accused, but a majority of two was needed to find against the accused.

B. In civil cases the judges could change their judgment in favor of either party. In criminal cases they could reverse their judgment in order to find *for* but not *against* the convict.

C. In civil cases all the judges could argue for either party. In criminal cases they could all argue to find *for* but not *against* the accused.

D. In civil cases a judge who argued against one party could later argue for the other, and vice versa. In criminal cases a judge who argued to convict could later argue to acquit but not vice versa.

E. In civil cases the opinions of the senior judges were expressed first. In criminal cases the opinions of the junior judges were expressed first to prevent them from being influenced by the opinion of their seniors.

12. If the accused was found guilty and was being led to the place of execution, there still was a provision on his behalf. As he was led to the place of execution a herald preceded him, calling out his name, his crime, when and where it was committed, and the names of those upon the basis of whose testimony he was condemned. The herald proclaimed that anyone who possesses any evidence favorable to the condemned should hasten to produce it.

Should such evidence be forthcoming or should the condemned man declare that he can prove his innocence a stay of execution was granted. If the convict's testimony proved to be ineffective, he was still allowed to make another attempt at proving himself innocent, since two scholars walked along with him for the purpose of judging whether any further testimony that he might offer would justify a delay in execution.

13. If the accused was acquitted he could not be placed in jeopardy a second time regardless of what new evidence might be forthcoming.

Sentiment Against Capital Punishment

It is quite clear that the many restrictions and provisions imposed by the Rabbis made it very difficult to inflict capital punishment. George Foot Moore, an eminent authority on Judaism, wrote in this connection: "It is clear that with such a procedure conviction in capital cases was next to impossible, and that this was the intention of the framers of the rules is equally plain." The sentiment against capital punishment is expressed in the Mishnah in an opinion which maintains that a court which executes one man in seven years is a destructive one. Rabbi Eleazar ben Azariah maintained that a court is destructive if it executes one man in seventy years. Rabbi Tarfon and Rabbi Akiba said, "If we had been in the Sanhedrin, no man would ever have been put to death" (Mishnab Makkot 1, 10).

From our discussion of the provisions and restrictions imposed by the Rabbis upon the procedure in the trial of capital cases, we believe that it is reasonable to maintain that they did not look with favor upon capital punishment.

The Moral Benefits of the Death Penalty

ERNEST VAN DEN HAAG

In the following article, Ernest van den Haag argues that capital punishment is morally justified. Van den Haag begins by citing the biblical mandate for harsh and irrevocable justice. He then considers how concepts such as charity and justice, human dignity, sanctity of life, and severity of punishment lend support to the use of the death penalty as a just retribution for murder. He concludes by declaring the importance of capital punishment in bringing justice to people responsible for murderous acts. Ernest van den Haag was one of the leading proponents of the death penalty and wrote widely on the topic from the 1960s until his death in 2002. He served as professor of jurisprudence and public policy at Fordham University and as a distinguished scholar at the Heritage Foundation, a public policy research institute.

Miscarriages of justice are rare, but do occur. Over a long enough time they lead to the execution of some innocents. Does this make irrevocable punishments morally wrong? Hardly. Our government employs trucks. They run over innocent bystanders more frequently than courts sentence innocents to death. We do not give up trucks because the benefits they produce outweigh the harm, including the death of innocents. Many human activities, even quite trivial ones, foreseeably cause wrongful deaths. Courts may cause fewer wrongful deaths than golf.

Ernest van den Haag, "The Death Penalty Once More," *University of California–Davis Law Review*, vol. 18, Summer 1985. Copyright © 1985 by the Regents of the University of California. Reproduced by permission.

Whether one sees the benefit of doing justice by imposing capital punishment as moral, or as material, or both, it outweighs the loss of innocent lives through miscarriages, which are as unintended as traffic accidents.

Some abolitionists feel that the motive for the death penalty is an un-Christian and unacceptable desire for vengeance. But though vengeance be the motive, it is not the purpose of the death penalty. Doing justice and deterring crime are the purposes, whatever the motive. Purpose (let alone effect) and motive are not the same.

The Lord is often quoted as saying "Vengeance is mine." He did not condemn vengeance. He merely reserved it to Himself—and to the government. For, in the same epistle He is also quoted as saying that the ruler is "the minister of God, a revenger, to execute wrath upon him that doeth evil." The religious notion of hell indicates that the biblical God favored harsh and everlasting punishment for some. However, particularly in a secular society, we cannot wait for the day of judgment to see murderers consigned to hell. Our courts must "execute wrath upon him that doeth evil" here and now.

Today many religious leaders oppose capital punishment. This is surprising, because there is no biblical warrant for their opposition. The Roman Catholic Church and most Protestant denominations traditionally have supported capital punishment. Why have their moral views changed? When sharing secular power, the churches clearly distinguished between justice, including penalization as deserved, a function of the secular power, and charity, which, according to religious doctrine, we should feel for all those who suffer for whatever reasons. Currently, religious leaders seem to conflate justice and charity, to conclude that the death penalty and, perhaps, all punishment, is wrong because uncharitable. Churches no longer share secular power. Perhaps bystanders are more ready to replace justice with charity than are those responsible for governing.

The Morality of Execution

Let me return to the morality of execution. Many abolitionists believe that capital punishment is "degrading to human dignity" and inconsistent with the "sanctity of life." Justice [William] Brennan, concurring in *Furman* [which held that the death is cruel and unusual punishment], stressed these phrases repeatedly. He did not explain what he meant.

Why would execution degrade human dignity more than life imprisonment? One may prefer the latter; but it seems at least as degrading as execution. Philosophers, such as Immanuel Kant and G.F.W. Hegel, thought capital punishment indispensable to redeem, or restore, the human dignity of the executed. Perhaps they were wrong. But they argued their case, whereas no one has explained why capital punishment degrades. Apparently those who argue that it does degrade dignity simply define the death penalty as degrading. If so, degradation (or dehumanization) merely is a disguised synonym for their disapproval. Assertion, reassertion, or definition do not constitute evidence or argument, nor do they otherwise justify, or even explain, disapproval of capital punishment.

Writers, such as Albert Camus, have suggested that murderers have a miserable time waiting for execution and anticipating it. I do not doubt that. But punishments are not meant to be pleasant. Other people suffer greatly waiting for the end, in hospitals, under circumstances that, I am afraid, are at least as degrading to their dignity as execution. These sufferers have not deserved their suffering by committing crimes, whereas murderers have. Yet, murderers suffer less on death row, unless their consciences bother them.

Some writers insist that the suffering the death penalty imposes on murderers exceeds the suffering of their victims. This is hard to determine, but probably true in some cases and not in other cases. However, the comparison is irrelevant. Murderers are punished, as are all offenders, not just for the suffering they caused their victims, but for the harm they do to society by making life insecure, by threatening everyone, and by requiring protective measures. Punishment, ultimately, is a vindication of the moral and legal order of society. . . .

The Sanctity of Life

We are enjoined by the Declaration of Independence to secure life. How can this best be achieved? The Constitution authorizes us to secure innocent life by taking the life of murderers, so that any one who deliberately wants to take an innocent life will know that he risks forfeiting his own. The framers did not think that taking the life of a murderer is inconsistent with the "sanctity of life" which Justice Brennan champions. He has not indicated why they were wrong.

Ever since Cesare Bonesana [eighteenth-century death penalty abolitionist], Marchese di Beccaria, wrote *Dei Delitti e Delle Pene* [On Crimes and Punishments], abolitionists have contended that executing murderers legitimizes murder by doing to the murderer what he did to his victim. Indeed, capital punishment retributes, or pays back the offender. Occasionally we do punish offenders by doing to them what they did to their victims. We may lock away a kidnapper who wrongfully locked away his victim, and we may kill the murderer who wrongfully killed his victim. To lawfully do to the offender what he unlawfully did to his victim in no way legitimizes his crime. It legitimizes (some) killing, and not murder. An act does not become a crime because of its physical character, which, indeed, it may share with the legal punishment, but because of its social, or, better, antisocial, character—because it is an unlawful act.

Severity of Punishment

Is the death penalty too severe? It stands in a class by itself. But so does murder. Execution is irreparable. So is murder. In contrast, all other crimes and punishments are, at least partly or potentially, reparable. The death penalty thus is congruous with the moral and material gravity of the crime it punishes.

Still, is it repulsive? Torture, however well deserved, now is repulsive to us. But torture is an artifact. Death is not, since nature has placed us all under sentence of death. Capital punishment, in [philosopher] John Stuart Mill's phrase, only "hastens death"—which is what the murderer did to his victim. I find nothing repulsive in hastening the murderer's death, provided it be done in a nontorturous manner. Had he wished to be secure in his life, he could have avoided murder.

To believe that capital punishment is too severe for any act, one must believe that there can be no act horrible enough to deserve death. I find this belief difficult to understand. I should readily impose the death penalty on a Hitler or a Stalin, or on anyone who does what they did, albeit on a smaller scale.

Symbolic Significance

The death penalty has become a major issue in public debate. This is somewhat puzzling, because quantitatively it is insignificant. Still, capital punishment has separated the voters as a whole from a small, but influential, abolitionist elite. There are, I believe, two reasons that explain the prominence of the issue.

First, I think, there is a genuine ethical issue. Some philosophers believe that the right to life is equally imprescriptible for all, that the murderer has as much right to live as his victim. Others do not push egalitarianism that far. They believe that there is a vital difference, that one's right to live is lost when one intentionally takes an innocent life, that everyone has just the right to one life, his own. If he unlawfully takes that of another he, *eo ipso*, loses his own right to life.

Second, and perhaps as important, the death penalty has symbolic significance. Those who favor it believe that the major remedy for crime is punishment. Those who do not, in the main, believe that the remedy is anything but punishment. They look at the causes of crime and conflate them with compulsions, or with excuses, and refuse to blame. The majority of the people are less sophisticated, but perhaps they have better judgment. They believe that everyone who can understand the nature and effects of his acts is responsible for them, and should be blamed and punished, if he could know that what he did was wrong. Human beings are human because they can be held responsible, as animals cannot be. In that sense the death penalty is a symbolic affirmation of the humanity of both victim and murderer.

Michigan's Moral Stand Against the Death Penalty

EUGENE G. WANGER

In 1846 Michigan abolished the death penalty by law, becoming the first state to do so. In 1964 the state adopted an amendment to its constitution prohibiting the practice of capital punishment. In the following selection, attorney Eugene G. Wanger describes the history of the abolition of the death penalty in Michigan, including the adoption of the constitutional amendment banning it. Wanger drafted the following language contained in the historic document: "No law shall be enacted providing for the penalty of death." Wanger is a member of the federal bars and the state bar of Michigan. He is also the cochair of the Michigan Committee Against Capital Punishment.

S everal years ago a legislator in Texas was asked if he would vote to abolish capital punishment. "No," he replied, "capital punishment was good enough for my father and it's good enough for me."

That could not have happened in Michigan, for our state, by statute in 1846, was the first government in the English-speaking world to abolish capital punishment for murder and lesser crimes. Our state has never restored it. Since 1964, Michigan's constitution has prohibited it.

Today [2002], following Michigan's lead, a majority of all

Eugene G. Wanger, "Michigan and Capital Punishment," *Michigan Bar Journal*, vol. 81, September 2002, pp. 38–41. Copyright © 2002 by Eugene G. Wanger. Reproduced by permission of the publisher and the author.

the nations on earth—including Canada, Mexico, England, Scandinavia, and almost all of Europe—have abolished the death penalty, either de jure or de facto; but America (with exception of Michigan and 12 other states) is one of the world's principal executing nations. Since 1998, only China and the [Republic of] Congo have executed more people than the United States. Iraq and Iran are not far behind.

What has created this unique and paradoxical situation? How did Michigan come to abolish the death penalty so early [1846], and how has that position been maintained?

Executions in Europe

The initial inspiration seems to have come from the eighteenth-century European Enlightenment. That was a time when the criminal law of civilized countries everywhere was ferocious, imposing torture and death for dozens—and in England as many as 200—of even the most trivial crimes.

Human life was cheap, especially if it was the life of the lowly. Executions were common entertainment. Men and sometimes women were executed without qualms and with dispatch, normally after rapid and perfunctory proceedings. As [the poet] Alexander Pope said,

> The hungry Judges soon the Sentence sign,
> And Wretches hang the Jury-men may Dine.

Does all of this seem to you like a very long time ago? Then talk to Bette Hulbert, recently retired director of the Michigan Historical Museum, who remembers her great-grandmother telling her of being taken when she was a little schoolgirl in Northern France to the center of town with the other children to see a man have his limbs each tied to one of four "big white horses" that then "just kept going" until they pulled him apart.

> Put the scaffold on the Commons,
> Where the multitude can meet;
> All the schools and ladies summon,
> Let them all enjoy the treat.

In London, where picking pockets was a hanging offense, pickpockets plied their trade with greatest success at the public hangings, when everyone else was "looking up"; and as late as 1807, at a triple hanging outside the Old Bailey [London's Central Criminal Court], the pressure of the crowd to see the final struggles of the condemned was so great that 30 of the spectators were crushed to death at the foot of the gallows. A publication of the time even gives their names and addresses.

In combating these and other evils for almost a hundred years, the philosophes, as the leaders of the Enlightenment were called, assiduously promoted a highly critical attitude toward the authority of the past and inculcated a powerfully optimistic view that the lot of humanity could be vastly improved through the application of human reason.

When the ideas of the Enlightenment swept across the Atlantic Ocean, they became well known to the leaders of the American Colonies. Here, unlike in England, there were only about a dozen crimes punishable by death. And here in the Colonies it troubled many to think, or be told, that among other things the death penalty might violate fundamental principles of Christianity.

Death Penalty Abolition Movement in America

The death penalty abolition campaign was begun by the American patriot, staunch Christian, signer of the Declaration of Independence, and eminent physician, Benjamin Rush of Philadelphia. He was the first American to speak out against the penalty of death for murder, which he did in a paper he read at Benjamin Franklin's house on March 9, 1787, and in an essay published in the *American Museum* magazine for July of the following year.

Rush widely distributed these essays and the campaign to abolish the death penalty in America was on. Many brilliant and talented reform leaders joined the fray, concentrating mainly in New England, New York, and Pennsylvania. The first success, however, was achieved in the wilds of Michigan. Peopled largely by immigrants from New York and New England, and with little experience of executions, Michigan Territory held a disagreeably traumatic hanging in Detroit in 1830. The following January, Governor Lewis Cass—still considered Michigan's greatest public servant—told the Territory's Legislative Council, "The period is probably not far distant, when it will be universally acknowledged, that all the just objects of human laws may be fully answered, without the infliction of capital punishment."

Capital Punishment in Michigan

Four years later, Michigan initially grappled with the capital punishment question when writing its first state Constitution in 1835. On the fourth day of the Constitutional Convention, one committee proposed a constitution stating in part, "Capital punishment ought not to be inflicted; the true design of all punishment being to reform, not to exterminate mankind."

But the proposal was not adopted, and a prevailing sentiment in the brief debate appeared to be that the state was as yet unprepared to "make all necessary and adequate provision for the safe and sure confinement of criminals." Michigan's capital punishment abolitionists, however, would soon be back.

The next few years saw them conduct several legislative skirmishes without result, and in about 1840, Michiganians learned that the Canadians had hanged an innocent man three years before just across the river in what is now Windsor, the true culprit later having made a death-bed confession of his guilt.

In 1844, a joint committee of the Michigan Senate and House issued a report urging that the death penalty be abolished, but the committee's minority disagreed and the House sided with them by a vote of 34 to 10. In the report a substantial space is devoted to whether government has the theoretical right to impose the death penalty, a question involving the fundamental nature of government itself. Such basic questions were much on the minds of our American forebears as they settled this new land.

It is interesting that both sides went out of their way to support the religious argument (the majority taking over a page to do so), while at the same time saying that it was not really relevant to the debate. This argument, which was a dominant theme in the capital punishment abolition movement, generally pitted the hopeful injunctions of the four Christian Gospels against the ancient and somber poetry of Genesis 9:6, which advises, "Whoso sheddeth man's blood, by man shall his blood be shed."

The [death penalty] abolitionist majority barely mentioned the deterrence argument at all, although they could have cited a number of authorities from the Eastern States. On the other hand, the committee minority, who favored the death penalty, expressly rested their entire case on the deterrence argument.

Life Imprisonment for Murder

In 1846, victory in Michigan was at hand as the legislature undertook a general revision of all the state's laws, including its lengthy criminal code. The state's determined capital punishment abolitionists were ready. . . .

Getting rid of "death" for first-degree murder was more easily said than done, but after much skirmishing, that penalty was finally fixed at "solitary confinement at hard labor in the state prison for life." As long-time political observer and retired Wayne County judge James Lincoln said, it looked like the Senate held the whole criminal code hostage until the House came around. One enthusiastic supporter from the Eastern States reported, "The sun has risen in the West!"

Shortly afterwards, a condemned murderer awaiting execution at Michigan's new prison in Jackson was pardoned when the death-bed confession of the real killer showed he was innocent and the new law providing for life imprison-ment for murder instead of death became effective on March 1, 1847.

How did this remarkable, unprecedented change hap-pen? In the absence of better evidence, we seem to be forced back upon the eighteenth-century proposition that these abolitionists, following the tradition of the Enlight-enment, were rational people who simply took the argu-ments and evidence for capital punishment, weighed them in the balance of human reason, and found them wanting. If this is so, the implications are profound.

Capital Punishment and the Michigan Constitution

Four years after capital punishment was abolished, Michi-gan held its second constitutional convention. The "Con-Con" of 1850 was the first Michigan public body to have its debates reported verbatim and several of them were lively. A committee proposed that the death penalty be prohib-ited, but the proposal was rejected.

The arguments most often voiced were that the subject should be left to the legislature and that including it in the constitution would cause the people to reject the docu-ment. . . .

Between 1846 and the end of the century, several efforts to restore capital punishment in Michigan met with no suc-cess and the state's officials were frequently asked for their views. . . . Letters from several Michigan prison officials were published confirming that Michigan's abolition had not raised the murder rate.

In 1881, an elderly black woman, perhaps Michigan's all-time greatest fighter for human rights, the famed Sojourner Truth, told Michigan's legislature, which was then about to vote on whether to bring the death penalty back, "We are the makers of murderers if we do it." And in 1891, Michi-gan's greatest judge and legal scholar, the internationally renowned Thomas M. Cooley, wrote:

> The fundamental objection to the taking of human life by law is found in the tendency to destroy in men's minds the sense of the sacredness of life and to accustom them to regard without fear or horror its destruction.... Mankind are not to be impressed with the priceless value of existence by spectacles of deliberate executions, and so long as the state justifies the taking of life for crime against society, individuals will frame in their own minds excuses for taking it for offenses real or imaginary against themselves, or will take it without excuse when it stands in the way of their desires.

Sojourner Truth had said it all in 10 words the decade before.

The death penalty wasn't even mentioned at Michigan's constitutional convention of 1908. But as the flapper era dawned and prohibition put bootlegging on a business-like basis, crime rates began to rise. An irate Michigan legislature passed a death penalty bill with a referendum provision in 1931, which was soundly rejected by a vote of the people. Frank Murphy [former mayor of Detroit, governor of Michigan, and justice of the U.S. Supreme Court] and [automotive industry pioneer] Henry Ford were among the notable Michiganians against it.

By 1956, the Michigan House or Senate had voted eight times for capital punishment during the twentieth century. As the sixth decade of the century approached, voices began to be heard that Michigan's much-amended 1908 state constitution should be revised, and 144 delegates were elected by the people to a constitutional convention for that purpose in 1961.

Michigan's Constitution Forbids Death Penalty

Although the state's electorate was equally divided between the two major parties, two-thirds of the delegates it elected were Republican, most very conservative. So far as is known, neither the candidates nor anyone else had suggested that capital punishment was a subject for constitutional treatment. Certainly it had never entered the mind of the convention's youngest Republican delegate [this article's author Eugene Wanger] who was elected from the city of Lansing.

Ignorant of almost all the foregoing history, this delegate, only three years a lawyer, inspired by a law journal article on the death penalty that he picked up at law school and now found in his file, drafted a proposal—the only one on the subject as it turned out—which by an unusual turn came before the committee he was on. He drafted the final language, wrote the committee report, and even organized the floor debate supporting it. It passed the convention with only three dissenting votes. The statement that "No law shall be enacted providing for the penalty of death," became part of the Michigan constitution [in 1964].

Eight years later, the United States Supreme Court decided *Furman v. Georgia*, finding the death penalty as then administered in America to be unconstitutional. In another four years, the Supreme Court decided *Gregg* [*v. Georgia*], legalizing that penalty under different procedures. During all these years, the crime rates had been rising and the public suddenly seemed more frustrated, fearful, and angry than it had been in a long time.

Calls for restoring the death penalty in Michigan were heard and after the proponents of execution failed in the legislature, the first of four statewide petition drives was started to repeal the constitutional ban. The State Board of Canvassers and the courts, however, aided by the volunteer legal services of election law expert Tom Downs, determined that the petitions lacked sufficient signatures. About three years ago [1999], another try was made in the legislature that resoundingly failed, and Michigan's historic ban of capital punishment remains.

Over the decades, more than a dozen principal arguments have been made against the death penalty in America; but for the past few years, most of the attention seems to be concentrating upon these three:

1. It now appears to be a moral certainty, especially in the light of recent DNA evidence, that we are occasionally executing the innocent.

2. Around the world, and especially in Europe, capital punishment is increasingly viewed as a violation of basic international human rights.

3. The death penalty in the modern world is being seen as contrary to fundamental principles of religion. Not only many Christian leaders, but also many Jewish and some Muslim leaders, have joined in this view.

In so controversial an area it is always good to find common ground. Most people would agree with the proposition that no question of public policy, except peace and war, is more important than whether or not, or under what circumstances, government should be authorized by its citizens to kill people. After all, in a democracy, where the people are sovereign, when the government kills, it kills for you.

Chronology

1700s B.C.
The Babylonian Code of Hammurabi mandates the death penalty for a variety of crimes.

A.D. 30
The crucifixion of Jesus Christ occurs. This is considered by many to be the state-sanctioned killing that has had the most profound effect on Western civilization.

1500s
In the early English criminal justice system, capital crimes are limited to seven offenses: arson, burglary, larceny, petty treason (murder of a husband by the wife), rape, robbery, and treason.

Early 1600s
English colonies in North America establish capital punishment for various crimes.

1608
The first colonist is executed; the hanging occurs in Jamestown.

1682
Cruel and unusual punishment is forbidden by the English bill of rights.

1764
Italian jurist Cesare Beccaria publishes his treatise *On Crimes and Punishments.*

1789

Joseph-Ignace Guillotin designs a machine, the guillotine, that offers the criminal justice system of his day a more humane form of execution.

1791

The Bill of Rights—the first ten amendments to the U.S. Constitution—is adopted. The Eighth Amendment's prohibition against cruel and unusual punishment will be used in later court cases to test the validity of capital punishment statutes and methods.

1833

Edward Livingston's article "Introductory Report to the System of Penal Law Prepared for the State of Louisiana" proposes that the death penalty be abolished in Louisiana.

1845

The first national organization of death penalty abolitionists—the American Society for the Abolition of Capital Punishment—meets in Philadelphia.

1847

Michigan is the first state to abolish the death penalty.

1868

The Fourteenth Amendment to the U.S. Constitution is adopted. Its "due process" and "equal protection" clauses will be used in later court cases to test the validity of death penalty statutes.

1879

The U.S. Supreme Court ruling in *Wilkerson v. Utah* holds that the public execution of a convicted murderer is not a violation of the Eighth Amendment's cruel and unusual punishment clause.

1890

The U.S. Supreme Court ruling in the *In re Kemmler* case states that the death penalty is not cruel and unusual punishment. The Court also approves the use of the electric chair.

1910

The U.S. Supreme Court rules in *Weems v. United States* that what constitutes cruel and unusual punishment is subject to change over time.

1924

In an execution in the state of Nevada, a gas chamber is used for the first time.

1925

Death in the electric chair is substituted for hanging for federal capital offenses.

1932

In *Powell v. Alabama*, the U.S. Supreme Court holds that due process requires that defendants be assigned adequate counsel.

1939

The Legal Defense Fund (LDF) is started by the National Association for the Advancement of Colored People. The LDF will defend numerous African Americans in capital cases and make many constitutional challenges to capital punishment.

1946

President Harry Truman, in conjunction with the War Department, puts limits on capital punishment from military courts-martial.

1953

Ethel and Julius Rosenberg are executed after being convicted of espionage. They are the first civilians to be put to death for that crime.

1963

Victor Feuger, hanged for kidnapping, is the last federal defendant to be put to death in the United States until 2001.

1967

Luis Jose Monges is executed in the gas chamber in the state of Colorado. Because of constitutional questions about the use of capital punishment, Monges is the last defendant put to death until 1977.

1968

In *Witherspoon v. Illinois*, the U.S. Supreme Court holds that potential jurors who are against capital punishment cannot be kept off of a jury for that reason.

1972

The Supreme Court rules in *Furman v. Georgia* that the imposition of the death penalty constitutes cruel and unusual punishment.

1976

The Supreme Court rules in *Gregg v. Georgia* that the imposition of the death penalty is not necessarily cruel and unusual punishment.

1977

In the first execution since 1967, Gary Gilmore is put to death by firing squad in the state of Utah.

1980

In *Godfrey v. Georgia*, the Supreme Court finds that overly broad capital punishment statutes are unconstitutional.

1986

The Supreme Court holds in *Ford v. Wainwright* that it is a violation of the Eighth Amendment to execute a person who is insane at the time of execution.

1987

The Supreme Court determines in *McCleskey v. Kemp* that a disparity in meting out death sentences between blacks and whites in Georgia does not make the state's death penalty statute unconstitutional.

1988

In *Thompson v. Oklahoma*, the Supreme Court rules that executing persons under the age of sixteen violates "civilized standards of decency" as well as the U.S. Constitution.

1995

The state of New York restores the death penalty.

2000

Illinois governor George Ryan decrees a moratorium on executions while announcing that the state's capital punishment system was not working to protect innocent defendants.

2001

In the first federal execution since 1963, Timothy McVeigh, convicted of murder, is put to death by lethal injection.

2002

Maryland governor Parris Glendening orders a moratorium on executions, citing racial unfairness. Reversing its 1987 decision of *Penry v. Lynaugh*, the U.S. Supreme Court rules that it is cruel and unusual punishment, in violation of the Eighth Amendment, to execute a mentally retarded person.

Organizations to Contact

The editors have compiled the following list of organizations concerned with the topics contained in this book. The descriptions are derived from materials provided by the organizations. All have publications or information available for interested readers. The list was compiled on the date of publication of the present volume; the information provided here may change. Be aware that many organizations take several weeks or longer to respond to inquiries, so allow as much time as possible.

Amnesty International USA
322 Eighth Ave., New York, NY 10001
(212) 807-8400 • fax: (212) 627-1451
Web site: www.amnesty-usa.org

Amnesty International is an independent worldwide movement working impartially for the release of all prisoners of conscience, for fair and prompt trials for political prisoners, and for an end to torture and executions. AI is funded by donations from its members and supporters throughout the world. AI has published several books and reports, including *Fatal Flaws: Innocence and the Death Penalty.*

Canadian Coalition Against the Death Penalty (CCADP)
80 Lillington Ave., Toronto, ON M1N 3K7 Canada
(416) 693-9112
e-mail: info@ccadp.org • Web site: www.ccadp.org

The CCADP is a not-for-profit international human rights organization dedicated to educating on alternatives to the death penalty worldwide and to providing emotional and practical support to death row inmates, their families, and the families of murder victims. The center releases pamphlets and periodic press releases, and its Web site includes a student resource center providing research information on capital punishment.

Capital Punishment Project
American Civil Liberties Union (ACLU)
125 Broad St., 18th Fl., New York, NY 10004
(212) 549-2585 • fax: (212) 549-2647
Web site: www.aclu.org

The project is dedicated to abolishing the death penalty. The ACLU believes that capital punishment violates the Constitution's ban on cruel and unusual punishment as well as the requirements of due process and equal protection under the law. It publishes and distributes numerous books and pamphlets, including *The Case Against the Death Penalty* and *Frequently Asked Questions Concerning the Writ of Habeas Corpus and the Death Penalty.*

Death Penalty Information Center (DPIC)
1320 Eighteenth St. NW, 5th Fl., Washington, DC 20036
(202) 293-6970 • fax: (202) 822-4787
e-mail: jrdeans@deathpenaltyinfo.org
Web site: www.deathpenaltyinfo.org

The DPIC conducts research into public opinion on the death penalty. The center believes capital punishment is discriminatory and excessively costly and that it may result in the execution of innocent persons. It publishes numerous reports, such as *Millions Misspent: What Politicians Don't Say About the High Costs of the Death Penalty, Innocence and the Death Penalty: Assessing the Danger of Mistaken Executions*, and *With Justice for Few: The Growing Crisis in Death Penalty Representation.*

Justice Fellowship
1856 Old Reston Ave., Reston, VA 20190
(703) 904-7312 • (703) 904-7307
Web site: www.justicefellowship.org

This Christian organization bases its work for reform of the justice system on the concept of victim-offender reconciliation. It does not take a position on the death penalty.

Justice for All
9525 Katy Freeway, Houston, TX 77024
(713) 935-9300 • fax: (713) 935-9301
e-mail: info@jfa.net • Web site: www.jfa.net

Justice for All is a not-for-profit criminal justice reform organization that supports the death penalty. Its activities include circulating online petitions to keep violent offenders from being paroled early and publishing the monthly newsletter the *Voice of Justice*.

Lamp of Hope Project
PO Box 305, League City, TX 77574-0305
e-mail: ksebung@lampofhope.org
Web site: www.lampofhope.org

The project was established and is run primarily by Texas death row inmates. It works for victim-offender reconciliation and for the support of both victims' and prisoners' families. It publishes and distributes the periodic *Texas Death Row Journal*.

Lincoln Institute for Research and Education
1001 Connecticut Ave. NW, Suite 1135, Washington, DC 20036
(202) 223-5112

The institute is a conservative think tank that studies public policy issues affecting the lives of black Americans, including the issue of the death penalty, which it favors. It publishes the quarterly *Lincoln Review*.

NAACP Legal Defense and Education Fund
99 Hudson St., Suite 1600, New York, NY 10013
(212) 965-2200
Web site: www.naacpldf.org

Founded by the National Association for the Advancement of Colored People, the fund opposes the death penalty and works to end discrimination in the justice system. It compiles and reports statistics on the death penalty and publishes legal materials, fact sheets, and reports.

National Coalition to Abolish the Death Penalty
920 Pennsylvania Ave. SE, Washington, DC 20003
(202) 543-9577 • fax: (202) 543-7798
e-mail: kjones@ncadp.org • Web site: www.ncadp.org

The National Coalition to Abolish the Death Penalty is a collection of more than 115 groups working together to stop executions in the United States. The organization compiles statistics on the death penalty. To further its goal, the coalition publishes information packets, pamphlets, and research materials.

National Criminal Justice Reference Service
U.S. Department of Justice
PO Box 6000, Rockville, MD 20849-6000
(301) 519-5500 • (800) 851-3420 • fax: (301) 519-5212
e-mail: askncjrs@ncjrs.org • Web site: www.ncjrs.org

The National Criminal Justice Reference Service is one of the most extensive sources of information on criminal and juvenile justice in the world. For a nominal fee, this clearinghouse provides topical searches and reading lists on many areas of criminal justice, including the death penalty. It publishes an annual report on capital punishment.

National Organization of Parents of Murdered Children
100 E. Eighth St., Suite B-41, Cincinnati, OH 45202
(513) 721-5683 • fax: (513) 345-4489
e-mail: natlpomc@aol.com • Web site: www.pomc.com

This group provides support to families of homicide victims through educational and criminal justice advocacy programs. It also provides training to law, mental health, and social service professionals to learn more about survivor issues and concerns.

For Further Research

James P. Acker, Robert M. Bohm, and Charles S. Lanier, eds., *America's Experiment with Capital Punishment: Reflections on the Past, Present, and Future of the Ultimate Penal Sanction.* Durham, NC: Carolina Academic, 1998.

Amnesty International Publications, *When the State Kills . . . the Death Penalty: A Human Rights Issue.* New York: Amnesty International, 1989.

Johannes Andenaes, *Punishment and Deterrence.* Ann Arbor: University of Michigan Press, 1974.

Cesare Beccaria, *On Crimes and Punishments.* New York: Marsilio, 1996.

Hugo Adam Bedau, *The Courts, the Constitution, and Capital Punishment.* Lexington, MA: Lexington Books, 1977.

———, ed., *The Death Penalty in America.* Garden City, NY: Anchor Books, 1967.

———, ed., *The Death Penalty in America: Current Controversies.* New York: Oxford University Press, 1997.

Hugo Adam Bedau, Constance E. Putnam, and Michael L. Radelet, *In Spite of Innocence: Erroneous Convictions in Capital Cases.* Boston: Northeastern University Press, 1992.

Walter Berns, *For Capital Punishment: Crime and the Morality of the Death Penalty.* New York: BasicBooks, 1979.

Edwin M. Borchard, *Convicting the Innocent: Errors of Criminal Justice.* New Haven, CT: Yale University Press, 1932.

John F. Galliher et al., *America Without the Death Penalty.* Boston: Northeastern University Press, 2002.

Keith Harries, *The Geography of Execution: The Capital Punishment Quagmire in America*. Lanham, MD: Rowman & Littlefield, 1997.

Gordon Hawkins and Franklin E. Zimring, *Capital Punishment and the American Agenda*. Cambridge, UK: Cambridge University Press, 1986.

Morton J. Horitz and Stanley N. Katz, eds., *American Law: The Formative Years, Reform of Criminal Law in Pennsylvania: Selected Enquiries 1787–1819*. New York: Arno, 1972.

Margaret C. Jasper, *The Law of Capital Punishment*. Dobbs Ferry, NY: Oceana, 1998.

Barry Latzer, *Death Penalty Cases*. Boston: Butterworth-Heinemann, 1998.

David Lester, *The Death Penalty: Issues and Answers*. Springfield, IL: Charles C. Thomas, 1998.

Edward Livingston, *The Complete Works of Edward Livingston on Criminal Jurisprudence*. 2 vols. Montclair, NJ: Patterson Smith, 1968.

James J. Megivern, *The Death Penalty: An Historical and Theological Survey*. New York: Paulist Press, 1997.

Kent S. Miller and Michael L. Radelet, *Executing the Mentally Ill: The Criminal Justice System and the Case of Alvin Ford*. Newbury Park, CA: Sage, 1993.

Dagobert D. Runes, ed., *The Selected Writings of Benjamin Rush*. New York: Philosophical Library, 1947.

Gregory D. Russell, *The Death Penalty and Racial Bias: Overturning Supreme Court Assumptions*. Westport, CT: Greenwood, 1994.

Austin Sarat, *When the State Kills: Capital Punishment and the American Condition*. Princeton, NJ: Princeton University Press, 2001.

Ernest van den Haag, *The Death Penalty: A Debate.* New York: Plenum, 1983.

Carol Wekesser, ed., *The Death Penalty: Opposing Viewpoints.* San Diego: Greenhaven, 1991.

Welsh S. White, *The Death Penalty in the Nineties: An Examination of the Modern System of Capital Punishment.* Ann Arbor: University of Michigan Press, 1991.

James Q. Wilson, *Thinking About Crime.* New York: Vintage Books, 1985.

is necessary to protect
society, 103–108
is unfair and should be
abolished, 166–74
con, 151–55
as method of social
control, 144–50
moratorium on
ABA's call for, 166–68
growth in support for,
171–73
in Illinois, 171
spirit of *Furman* and,
173–74
symbolic significance of,
207–208
Declaration of Rights
(England, 1688), 27–28
Demby (slave), 145–46
Denno, Deborah W., 13
deterrence
is unacceptable rationale
for juvenile execution,
66–67
as purpose for death
penalty, 54–55, 107–108
argument against, 99
DiIulio, John J., 153
Dlugash, Melvin, 142
DNA evidence, 122
assures fairness of death
penalty, 175–77
death row inmates freed by,
171
Douglas, William O., 38, 39
Douglass, Frederick, 145, 146
Downs, Tom, 216
Duffy, Clifton, 16
Duncan, Elizabeth, 157
Durkheim, Émile, 77

Eddings v. Oklahoma (1982),
65
Ehrlich, Isaac, 113, 115–18
Eighth Amendment, 20
application of
in *Furman v. Georgia,* 39
in *McCleskey v. Kemp,* 124,
128–29
to states, 27
execution of the mentally
retarded does not violate,
21
human dignity as core of,
53, 75–76
electrocution
introduction of, 15–16
is not cruel and unusual
punishment, 22–29
New York statute providing
for, 25–26
Ellis, Vernon, 142
Enlightenment, 210–11
Enmund v. Florida (1982), 64
execution
colonial methods of, 13–14
in Europe, 210–11
means of, and evolving
standards of decency, 45
morality of, 205–206

Federal Bureau of
Investigation (FBI), 154
Feingold, Russ, 173
Fifth Amendment,
contemplates capital
punishment, 69, 72–73
firing squad, 15
Ford, Henry, 215
Ford v. Wainwright (1986), 21
Fourteenth Amendment
application of